Whether you're a manage: or someone searching f~~_ difference~~ personally, professionally, politically or philanthropically, this book will help you flex and grow leadership and brand building muscles for more impact in everything you do.

Leadership and branding is a journey, not a destination. It can be messy, difficult and frustrating. It can be lonely, scary and uncharted. But it can also be fun, fruitful and extremely fulfilling. Leadership and confidence are powerful keys to building trust and transforming not just your life but the lives of others. When women choose to lead, they will rise from invisible to invincible, they will inspire others, and together they will disrupt problems and affect lasting change. If you want to be that kind of woman, I highly recommend you use Amanda's book as your road map; it will ignite and fuel your journey.

Dr. Jackie Freiberg, author, speaker, ex-coach and certified Dare to Lead™ facilitator

Women tend to have a natural tendency to over-prove when it comes to showcasing their expertise and value to business. This often leads to missed promotions and missed opportunities. *Invisible to Invincible* provides great insights into why this happens as well as practical ways for women to self-promote in a way that is authentic to them. A must-read book for women who want to achieve career success … and for men who want to support women to achieve their full potential.

Gabrielle Dolan, international speaker, best-selling author of five books including Real Communication: How to be you and lead true

Effective communication about the difference you've made (self-promotion) is crucial to success. Amanda Blesing's wisdom and guidance in *Invisible to Invincible* enables women to develop, strengthen and deploy this essential career skill.

Susan Colantuono, CEO and founder of Leading Women, author of No Ceiling, No Walls and Make the Most of Mentoring

If you've ever felt sick to your stomach at the thought of networking and selling 'brand you' then this book is worth reading. Amanda's deep understanding of the challenges and pitfalls for executive women is unique and once you absorb the wisdom in these pages, you'll be ready, willing and eager to self-promote with the best of them.

Repa Patel, speaker, facilitator, coach, mindful leadership

Co-create your own future. This is not woo woo, fluffy advice on how to succeed in an executive career; it's a practical call to action for executive women everywhere. I've worked with Amanda over several years and her advice has been invaluable. If you want to lead and succeed, this book will show you how.

Alessandra Edwards, CEO of Performance Genome

As a woman wearing many (fabulous) hats (an executive leading a company in the software and construction industry; a member of several business and not-for-profit organisations; a committed family devotee; and an exercise enthusiast) self-promotion was not something I prioritised. And hailing from the UK where tall-poppy syndrome is rife, it isn't natural for me to big-note myself. I've now worked with Amanda for several years and can say 'hand on heart' that the tactics she writes about in this book absolutely work. If you're an executive woman who is serious about your career, this is a must-read.

Carla Wall, managing director of Coins

From Invisible to Invincible demystifies self-promotion for executive women; it unpacks challenges and assumptions, then lays out an easy-to-follow road map. Amanda has been helping executive women win remuneration and recognition for many years, and this book captures her own authentic brand along with strategies and tactics that truly work.

Jane Anderson, award winning coach and content strategist, author and speaker

Amanda Blesing is well known in the women-in-leadership space, teaching and inspiring executive women how to get noticed for all the right reasons. Her advice tackles the issues of confidence, bias and stereotypes in a humorous and easy-to-read way. With case studies that bring lessons to life, and self-assessment tools that provoke action, *Invisible to Invincible* is an extraordinary gift to women leaders. It is more than just a leadership book; it's a comprehensive leadership toolkit.

Rachael Robertson, leadership and teamwork speaker, author and expert

As a world expert in negotiation and leadership, and a particular focus on gender equity, I love Amanda's practical approach to self-promotion for executive women. This book provides a thorough understanding of the challenges for women with leadership goals and aspirations, then provides a much needed road map to help them navigate more easily.

Carrie Gallant, leadership coach and 'Art of Negotiation for Women' expert

Invisible to Invincible

INVISIBLE TO
INVINCIBLE

A self-promotion
handbook for
executive women

AMANDA BLESING

A catalogue record for this book is available from the National Library of Australia

IISBN: 978-0-6482812-6-9

Typeset and printed in Australia by BookPOD
Cover design by Louise Williams
Edited by Joanna Yardley

Disclaimer

ABOUT THE AUTHOR

Approximately 25 years ago, Amanda began working her way through the ranks of association management; her last role was as CEO of SOCAP Australia (Society of Consumer Affairs Professionals Australia). While Amanda has a strong understanding of how to turn an organisation around, her expertise and passion remains in designing programs that help women to lead and succeed.

As the creator of The Ambition Revolution program, she currently speaks and consults with smart and savvy executive women. What really switches her on is seeing these individuals step up, speak out and take charge of their roles, careers, aspirations and their organisations.

What differentiates Amanda from the crowd is that despite humble origins she has big dreams; she is determined, self-assured and provides a great example of 'hands on' leadership that navigates the stormy waters between likeability and getting things done. She truly understands and provides solutions for the challenges people face in balancing a demanding role, ambition, and workload, so they can have a fulfilling personal life.

Amanda works one-on-one with executive level clients and runs corporate workshops on impact, branding and influence. Her first book, *Step Up, Speak Out, Take Charge: A woman's guide to getting ahead in your career* was published in 2016. *Invisible to Invincible* takes the reader even further.

Contents

#SELFPROMOTIONMATTERS

As women, we've been socialised to not 'big note' ourselves. Yet owning and sharing our expertise is key to a successful career. If we do stand out, it's usually because we are looking good, being gracious or glamorous, and never raising a sweat. Yet the key to kicking BHAGs (big hairy audacious goals) is to put ourselves out there.

The social penalty for women who self-promote and get it wrong, can be debilitating. We're so very attuned to that risk because we've been hearing criticisms and advice about standing out or fitting in for most of our lives.

I run my own business. I have to self-promote daily in order to stay successful. I struggle as much as the next person, especially when I'm tired or feeling vulnerable. The biggest lesson I've learned in this journey is to take 'self' out of self-promotion. Instead, focus on your 'why'—a sense of purpose or a cause. Not only will you find it easier, but you will be criticised less.

For the thousands who put yourselves out there every day in the face of possible criticism or rejection ... I respect you. Together, we are setting the scene for future generations to tackle things differently.

My goal, in writing this book, is to share tactics that deliver the biggest bang for their buck, the biggest ROI, or the Goldilocks Sweet Spot where the amount is not too much, not too little, but just right. No more going to the wrong networking functions over and over again because you think you should. No more daily (over) posting on LinkedIn because you've seen others do it—unless that really works for you. No more coffee highs from endless meetings with all and sundry under the guise of 'it's a numbers game', unless you know that coffee meetings really work or you are meeting with decision makers.

We know from research that executive women, in particular, struggle with self-advocacy, self- promotion and owning and claiming their expertise. So learning to skilfully activate self-promotion tactics that successfully navigate perception and bias (that actually work) may just be the winning strategy you need right now in your career.

INTRODUCTION

Self-promotion can indeed feel like it sucks

It feels bad for most; it can be incredibly uncomfortable. It looks 'icky' when we see someone get it wrong or when we perceive they have got it wrong because it goes against what you believe to be the norm. We feel bad for that person, but we may also experience a small voice on our shoulder that says 'Serves them right! Who do they think they are?'

We've all experienced that moment of *schadenfreude*, when we see someone who we believed to be big noting themselves, get their comeuppance. Or conversely, we assume that we're simply not as good as them because they were 'big noting' themselves with such confidence that we assumed they knew more.

What a 'self-promotion' conundrum—damned if you do, doomed if you don't. I know it intimately. I grew up in rural South Australia in a Protestant family who was diligent about religious practices including regular worship, Sunday school, youth groups, pastoral activities and church related social activities during the week. Don't get me wrong, there were definite benefits but there was also a downside. And that downside for me was my interpretation of the teachings around humility.

Humility is overrated

The notion of humility was drummed into me from an early age. Do great work, but don't expect credit for it. Dress to fit in, not to stand out (or only a little bit, certainly not flashy). Don't draw attention to yourself, wait for credit to find you and even then, be demure and take no pride in your success because your talents 'came from Jesus' anyway so they aren't yours to take pride in. Seeking credit for good deeds or great work was frowned upon. 'Pride goeth before a fall' was a common refrain. For those who did seek credit, the fear of social censure for doing so, by others in that same community, was always there.

Additionally, my mum was my school teacher. This alone came with a raft of benefits *and* downsides. She was always there to drive me and my siblings to school and we were super friendly with the school principal and his children. (Nothing like currying favour with the principal by proximity and familiarity!) Yet in her efforts to *not* show me any favours, she would ignore me if I put my hand up in class to answer a question; even when no-one else did, she'd pretend she hadn't seen me. While we laugh about this now, I remember becoming incredibly self-conscious, always worried about what other people thought of me. This agony of hyper self-awareness— always focused on the faults and areas for improvement, and never on the wins (I call it self-flagellation by self-awareness)—dogged me right through to my mid-20s.

It wasn't until the tender age of 25 that I experienced that 'aha' moment. I was working in the fitness industry in South Australia teaching aerobics, working reception and competing in State aerobics championships. There was a constant tension for me around putting myself out there to be the best fitness instructor I could be yet not taking credit where credit was due. Plus, I was becoming increasingly unhappy with my preoccupation with myself, which was in constant tension with the teachings that had permeated my younger years ensuring a focus less on self, more on others.

There I was struggling along one day at a time, trying desperately to reconcile my drive with the need for humility, when someone recommended I read *Fat is a Feminist Issue* by Susie Orbach (2006). It was then that I started to unpack and explore the ideas of humility, false humility, the passivity expected of 'the feminine', and modesty and societal expectations for women—all of which, in their own way, undermine confidence and keep women playing small.

Did that make self-promotion any easier? Heck no. These ideas were just the beginning of the journey for me. But I distinctly remember becoming angry with what I now know to be my misinterpretation of the term *humility*. How had I let myself be so deceived? And how had I wasted so much time and useless angst worrying about things that others didn't even consider?

Why? Because if we all *hid our light under a bushel* then nothing would be achieved. Human endeavour and development would be so much slower. We would not have leaders who inspired others to follow because those individuals would be deferring to someone else who might be more worthy. We would not have individuals who stood out and challenged the status quo when the status quo needed challenging, because those individuals might think it was not their place. And while word of mouth is a powerful marketing tool, at some point you have to be prepared to back yourself and speak out on your own behalf.

Then what happens? You get caught up in the busyness of life, doing the best you can with what you've got, carving a career path for yourself. When you're feeling fabulous, self-promotion tactics come a lot easier and more naturally. Yet when you're feeling stressed or blue the thought of self-promotion is right up there with going to the dentist—something you do once or twice a year under duress.

Spring forward 30 years and my life is one big self-promotion activity. I have my own name in my domain name. My website home page features a larger than life photo of me. (Note, it took me six months to get confident enough to do that). Go figure! When I first started my business, the first six months were dreadful. I went to networking function after networking function, attended coffee meeting after coffee meeting, and posted on LinkedIn three times per day in an attempt to get my name out there. All this resulted in me feeling tired, worthless and wondering if it were all worthwhile.

In desperation, I met with my mentor and posed the question, 'How do you not get tired and worn out going to networking functions?' She said, 'I don't go. If I want to attend a networking function, I host one'. In a nutshell, *she* found a way that kept her at her best, in front of the right people, on her own terms; whereas, *I* was allowing others to dictate the terms on which I engaged. I was giving other people control over my own destiny by remaining as a consumer of opportunity rather than a creator of opportunity. When I flicked the switch, things started happening.

I now purposefully blog and post to draw attention to the work I do (help executive women) but far less frequently than before. I relentlessly pursue opportunities to showcase my unique ideas but in alignment with my short- and long-term goals. I consistently put my name and ideas forward, whether they are wanted or not, because when I'm working with the right client, the benefits they gain are immense and that makes it all worthwhile.

Focus on the difference you make

How do I do this without feeling salesy? Well, I focus on the difference I make with my clients and know that if I can do this for one (me), then I can do it for others. In the month before Christmas of 2018 alone, I inspired two women to win increases of $90K+ on their salary packages, and another to win an increase of more than 30 per cent of her total package. Another woman told me she doubled her salary from the previous year as a result of working with me. In the months prior, I helped a client who had been in the same organisation for 22 years, to create an outward facing leadership brand for herself that enabled her to transition seamlessly and confidently into a new role in a new organisation. That's just a few ...

These results drive me. If I were to keep my skills and talents a secret because I was worried about how my self-promotion efforts would potentially be perceived, how could I help others? Am I better than others at self-promotion? Better than many and not as good as some, and I hate it along with everyone else. But I acknowledge that if I don't self-promote, the women who wouldn't get to know about me would be missing out.

(Un)common sense for self-promotors

Here are three key conundrums to start you on your self-promotion journey:

- Confidence matters: Research proves that our society confuses confidence with competence. You may be great at your job but if you don't behave as though you know that, others will assume you aren't good at your job.
- First impressions count: Researchers have found that people who act narcissistically and overly positive about themselves tend to make great first impressions. Seemingly, over-the- top self-promoters initially tend to come off positively. Others seem to like them and rate them as agreeable, competent, and well-adjusted. It's only if they continue to do this too much for too long that it has negative consequences. So don't sweat the small stuff especially when you first start your self-promotion journey.

- You aren't always the best judge so you need to learn to get out of your own way. Getting out of the way of your own ingrained beliefs, biases and default switches takes a lifetime of work.

This book was original titled *Noticed: For all the right reasons*. Oh how I loved that title. It was punchy. It was going to have a sealed section with 'all the wrong reasons' (and no, not *those* sort of wrong reasons. This was about relevance: the right audience, right message, right time, right place).

But when I reflected on the issues that many women face: a lack of agency or a tendency to rely more on waiting to be noticed than creating the notice, I simply could not go to print with that title. It would convey the *wrong* message after all.

Many of us were socialised with fairy stories and romance novels where the female protagonist waited to be rescued. If it weren't us, it was our mothers, grans, aunties, female cousins, babysitters or childcare workers who reared us with those same stereotypes in mind. This created a tendency towards a lack of agency. We ended up imagining that someone needed to invite us, for it to be worthwhile; that being *discovered* like *Australia's Top Model* is the holy grail (thank you *NOT Dolly Magazine*); and that somehow, if you actually created your own success then it wasn't as valid (as if someone else needed to make it happen for you). Logically, this doesn't even make sense, but it's so ingrained in the thinking of yesteryear that it's hard to decode or dismiss.

In 2015, I was attending an International Women's Day function and was seated at a table with a mature-aged (75+) business woman renowned in the dispute resolution sector. She had just published her first book. When I asked her why she waited so long to write the book, she replied 'No-one had invited me to write one before, so I didn't think it would be the right thing to do'. This exemplified much of what many women still think. They're still waiting to be invited. Think about what the world has missed out on …

Instead, we need to stop waiting and simply get on with the business of being great and creating a world we want to inhabit. Hence the importance of a book title that doesn't sound like we're waiting to be noticed, but instead, creating the notice ourselves.

My chosen book title *From Invisible to Invincible,* sounded far more colourful and playful and implies there is a process (which there is). Special thanks to Louise Williams, photographer and branding expert, who helped me embody my self-promotion IP far more powerfully. Yoga is something I have hidden from my leadership brand and kept 'invisible'; yet, it is a unique component of my brand. Becoming more authentic and showcasing these less visible components in a playful manner has made my message far more impactful.

I've chosen to start many of the chapters with a punchy mini blog in the style I use to post on LinkedIn. In fact, I've become something of an Accidental LinkedIn Ninja creating compelling content and viral blogs each week. They are vernacular in style, 1300 characters in length, utilise emojis and hashtags and are designed to capture attention—fast. I teach this style to my clients, and later in this book you'll read about executive women who reinvented themselves by posting and sharing via LinkedIn. For those who want to create a brand on LinkedIn, these mini blogs will give you an idea for how to structure your own compelling content with a propensity to go viral.

Finally, this book is designed so you can choose your own destination. If you want to get straight into the tactical and practical, head to Part 3. If you'd like to understand, more deeply, why you feel uncomfortable and what might be going on for you when you lean out of self-promotion type activities, be sure to read Part 1. It may even help you put some checks and balances in place so you aren't as impacted. Third, if you want a little more of the philosophy and methodology, so you can create tactics on your own, read Part 2.

Do get in touch if you come up with tactics you'd like to share with other executive women.

And to paraphrase Jennie Mustafa-Julock and Annie Passanisi, in *Self-Promotion Sucks (but it doesn't have to)* (Entrepreneurs, 2013), *let* the suck stop here.

PART 1

CHAPTER 1

IT'S TOUGH OUT THERE

Are you a #legend in your own #lunchbox? If not, why not?

In this era of #selfpromotion, you are your own marketing department and that requires a healthy dose of positive self-belief.

Self-belief > Self-confidence > Self-advocacy > Self-promotion > Legend in your own lunchbox.

The expression is 70s school yard trash talk for someone who has tickets on themselves or may just be too big for their own boots. But what if they are on the right track and this is exactly what's required to achieve and succeed?

You don't fly around the globe solo, #AmeliaEarhart style, if you don't believe in yourself; you can't become the most powerful female tennis player of all time, à la #SerenaWilliams, if you don't have healthy self-confidence; and you wouldn't become the 1st female PM in Australia (#JuliaGillard) if you didn't have positive self-belief.

You cannot lead a company if you aren't prepared to self-advocate, self-promote and to own and share your expertise. In a world that confuses confidence with competence, a bit of honest over confidence will go far.

Being a legend in your own lunchbox may simply be a prerequisite.

Who is in your lunchbox? A legend? Or someone who needs to do more work? And how do you get the balance right?

No-one likes self-promotion

No-one likes self-promotion. A Google search for 'how to self-promote without bragging' returns millions of hits because this is a problem for men and women alike. The social penalty and cost for getting it wrong can be unsettling and we all worry about negative fallout. No-one wants to be thought of as self-absorbed or narcissistic.

Tall Poppy Syndrome is alive and well here in Australia. Men and women worry that if they stand out for any reason, others will cut them down. No wonder the thought of blowing your own trumpet makes us feel uncomfortable. Yet we are all in the business of selling *something* whether we like it, know it, or are good at it.

- Career coaches are selling the benefits of levelling up in your career.
- Executives are selling the benefits of their executive function, division or department.
- Business leaders are busy selling the value of working in, purchasing from or investing in company X.

And you? You're selling the benefits of brand (insert your name here) personally and professionally. And the need to do so is only going to increase. Gone are the days when you turned up to work and put in the time to receive a pat on the back, promotion, and pay rise ... and then waited a (long) time until you marched towards the sweet release of a golden handshake and/or retirement.

In a globalised, digitised, fast changing world, it simply doesn't work that way. Data from the US Bureau of Labor Statistics suggests that the average person changes jobs an average of 12 times during his or her career. While in 2017, results from the Australian Bureau of Statistics told us that the average worker changed jobs 17 times in the course of their career and changed careers five times (Bureau of Labor Statistics).

With the rise of the portfolio career, careers by design, and the gig economy, where brand development is both for companies and individuals, you must stand out in a crowded employment marketplace in order to survive, let alone flourish. Purpose, passion and the opportunity to make your mark (or really make a difference) are attractive to most people.

> *'People who consider their work to be a calling tend to be more satisfied than those who think of their work as "just" a job.'*
>
> —Amy Wrzesniewski, Researcher, Yale School of Management

In first-world countries, it's no longer seen as a luxury to have a sense of purpose about your work. If spending most of your life at work, you may as well enjoy it and feel as though the work you are doing is contributing in some meaningful way.

So how do you survive?

You need to be proactively, strategically, and entrepreneurially putting yourself forward so that others know who you are and how you add value.

These days, even if you are planning your career inside one, two or three organisations, it's expected that you'll feel confident and capable enough to tap *yourself* on the shoulder and put *yourself* forward by identifying opportunities you'd like to tackle or areas where your expertise might provide more impact. It's expected you'll be entrepreneurial in nature and you'll know how to showcase your expertise to the right people, so you stand out for all the right reasons. There's no more waiting for others to find you; no more waiting for your boss to create opportunities for you. Everyone is the protagonist in their own movie, so you have the opportunity to take control of your own destiny and create a future you want to inhabit, rather than passively accepting the one that's mapped out for you.

Twenty years ago, we'd barely heard of personal branding for individuals. Ten years ago, we began to see the emergence of organisations who specialised in creating and refining personal brand strategies for celebrities and high-profile media personalities. Now, refining and honing your personal brand is part and parcel of leadership and the executive toolkit more broadly. It transcends notions of relying on old-school thinking around hard work, perfectionism and likeability in order to get ahead. It enables business leaders to develop their authentic voice and charisma and to create key messages and communications plans that deliver benefits inside the organisation and out to industry.

Let's take these ideas one step further and say that we also need to be strategic about it. It's not enough to simply spread yourself thin at networking functions and golf games. You need to focus on what's most effective, to separate busy from strategic and to focus on the areas that are going to give you the most bang for your buck and deliver on the results you need. Today, whether you are a business owner, a consultant, a professional in a firm, or on a fast track to corporate C-suite ascendancy, any strategy—even the wrong strategy—is better than no strategy. You need to be able to package everything up: you, your expertise, your results and what might be possible with you on board, so that others can find you and 'purchase' you more easily.

Four rules of thumb to remember:

- Work is not school: you won't get the corner office by being compliant or quiet.
- No-one promotes the stressed out, worn out and flustered looking executive with their head down backside up, hanging out at the back of the office.
- Results no longer speak for themselves.
- Strategy trumps busy—every day.

Accepting responsibility for taking charge of the narrative of your own career and success is a critically important first step. You need to see yourself as worthy of leading so that others see you in the same way. Help yourself to see past stereotypes and bias, which will in turn make it easier for others to see past their own biases and restrictions of stereotype that surround leadership.

It's not bragging when it's based on fact, is about real results, with real impact and outcomes, and for a purpose other than purely making yourself look good.

Finally, learn to fly your own flag for brand you. After all, there is nothing wrong with blowing your own trumpet, if you know how to play.

Women, leadership and visibility

I'm utterly gob-smacked that these attitudes exist in 2018

We have one woman already on the board, so we are done—it is someone else's turn.
All the 'good' women have already been snapped up.
Most women don't want the hassle or pressure of sitting on a board.

These statements were part of a list of the ten worst explanations given by CEOs of the 350 biggest publicly listed companies in Britain for low numbers of women serving on British boards, according to a *New York Times* article on 31 May 2018.

'As you read this list of excuses, you might think it's 1918 not 2018. It reads like a script from a comedy parody but it's true.'

~ Amanda Mackenzie, CEO, Business in the Community.

If you're in Australia thinking that we're different, think again. High profile male leaders recently expressed similar sentiments.

'You hear some of the blokes complaining but we are in the midst of a social revolution; now they have to compete against 100% of the population, not 50%.' ~ Ilana Atlas, Coca-Cola Amatil Chair.

Comments do not reflect research on the issue. Increasing numbers of investors are pushing for greater gender diversity on the boards.

What will it take to kick these attitudes to the kerb?

Throughout the globe, female leaders are still few and far between with *the 2018 McKinsey Women in the Workplace* report citing that the C-suite is *still* only made up of 19% of women despite concerted efforts by many. I emphasise *still* because this statistic hasn't changed in the four years of running this report.

In the Australian context, the WGEA reports that while women are finding board roles, the numbers of women achieving Csuite roles is still low. 'Despite the fact that women comprise almost 60% of university graduates and 46% of the workforce, only 10% of senior leaders and 4% of CEOs in Australian ASX200 companies are women'.

Is it a lack of talent? No, because research also proves that there is no real significant difference in intelligence and talent. In fact, 'the proportion of female postgraduates is higher than for undergraduates, accentuating the imbalance. Of the 42 universities in Australia, 35 have more female than male students with two having more than 70% females.' No shortage of talent there. (Larkins, 2018)

Is it a difference in ambition? Possibly. As I argue in my book *Step Up, Speak Out, Take Charge* (2016) men and women tend to value success and ambition differently. Masculine ambition is tied predominantly to financial gain while female ambition is more closely correlated to remuneration, being heard and making a difference. If women don't feel like they're being heard or making a difference, they are more likely to 'lean out', despite the money. A 2014 Bain & Company report indicates that women tend to 'lean out' more than men after just two years in an organisation. However, my guess is that this difference in ambition is only part of the issue. (Coffman & Neuenfeldt, 2014)

Is it a visibility issue? Absolutely. To quote Cindy Gallop, UK advertising agency executive, 'you cannot be who you cannot see'. There are so few women in the leadership stakes, that men and women the globe over don't see it as a natural or easy progression for women.

In *Women Rising: The Unseen Barriers* (Ibarra, Ely, & Kolb, 2013), one author had this to say about organisations who are creating opportunities and pathways for women but are not addressing the underlying issues around visibility and/or lack thereof:

> [regular programs] don't address the often fragile process of coming to see oneself, and to be seen by others, as a leader. Becoming a leader involves much more than being put in a leadership role, acquiring new skills, and adapting one's style to the requirements of that role. It involves a fundamental identity shift. Organisations inadvertently undermine this process when they advise women to proactively seek leadership roles without also addressing policies and practices that communicate a mismatch between how women are seen and the qualities and experiences people tend to associate with leaders.

Additionally, the media, television and advertising industries still rely on stereotypes to drive approval ratings and draw eyeballs, so women are not depicted as leaders and the perception is even more skewed. Relevantly, a recent global study of the advertising industry found that '... just 2% of adverts featured women who could be described as "intelligent"; just 3% were shown in leadership roles'. The advertising industry is just the tip of the iceberg with the media and entertainment industries, all such powerful influencers of our socialisation, compounding the problem and promoting and reinforcing a lack of 'visibility' for women as leaders.

Finally, and probably most significantly, *Harvard Business Review* published an article identifying that only 11% of case studies and text books in MBA and graduate leadership training programs feature women as leaders. Once again, it's challenging for anyone to see women as natural leaders when there is a dearth of visibility in the very texts that train our future leaders.

The flip side of lack of visibility is too much visibility. There is definitely a downside for those who become more visible, and it makes you vulnerable. The higher up the food chain you are, the more visible you become, particularly if you are unique or can identify as a minority. At best, being a female leader is viewed as unfeminine and at worst, it's viewed as taking jobs away from the blokes—this opens women up to criticism about their femininity.

The criticism is rarely about what women say or the content of key messages or even the results; it's frequently about:

- Our appearance and wardrobe choices.
- Our speech mannerisms.
- Whether we are nice enough.
- How we express our femininity.
- The way we manage our family obligations.
- How we articulate ambition.

In Australia, there is a history of personal attacks against senior female political figures. In recent years, we witnessed extremely personal attacks against former Prime Minister Julia Gillard by men and women, which prompted her world famous misogyny speech as a response. Additionally, if a female leader makes a mistake, it's as though she makes it on behalf of women everywhere, which becomes a burden and may increase her sense of vulnerability. The unprecedented attacks against Human Rights Commissioner Gillian Triggs were enough to put anyone off becoming more visible especially younger ambitious women who may have been considering a life in public office.

This is not limited to female politicians or office bearers, but to anyone in the public eye. You may remember the producers of Q&A on ABC in February 2016 discussing some of the challenges they experienced in getting women to appear on the show. These included the adversarial nature of the show, the dearth of women in public life, and the social media bullying and trolling that would likely eventuate.

While many of my clients don't work in public office, some work in the rarefied air of C-suite executive offices. They are extremely visible and, therefore, vulnerable, unless adequately prepared.

Visibility, aging and self-promotion

And finally, we can't talk about the issues of visibility for women without addressing the obvious gender bias around aging. The older a woman gets in our society, the more 'invisible' she becomes with some arguing the mysterious magical tipping point of 50 years old. After 50, women become 'less visible'. This is despite them being the ideal age of a leader and being more confident at this age. The opposite is true for men who are perceived as more credible and influential with age.

There is also the issue of socialisation, where mature women have not been socialised to self-promote as much as men or younger generations. Research released in 2014, revealed that senior women executives still struggle with some of the career advancement challenges of women in middle management. The research was the result of a survey of 326 senior women leaders across North America and the challenges that arose were:

- Selfpromotion
- Advocating for themselves
- Expressing their expertise.

Women have been socialised to believe that doing the job rigorously and thoroughly is a fast track to success and that their results and good work should speak for themselves. I hate to be the bearer of

bad news, but we got the wrong memo. As women in tl
we need to stand out and become more visible. We r
promote and be able to articulate our achievements b___. ...o tne
business with key messages about value. We also need to advocate
on our own behalf, not just on behalf of our team or junior staff.

The *2019 KPMG Women's Leadership Study: Risk, Resilience,
Reward* found that despite consistent advice to the contrary, women
still believe that career success comes from working hard and doing
the job well.

- 73% attributed to working hard.
- 45% said they were detailed oriented.
- 45% were well organised.
- 43% said they have talked about their accomplishments or
  raised their personal external visibility over the past three
  years.
- 24% said they were strong willed.
- 18% said they were creative.
- 17% said they were a good leaders.

Only 8% said risk taking has contributed most to their professional
success, crediting task-oriented factors over leadership traits.
Additionally, younger generations of men and women have grown
up in the era of celebrity and self-promotion. While older generations
may not be as comfortable with self-promotion tactics, younger
generations are skilfully executing self-promotion strategies,
advocating on their own behalf and claiming expert status far more
skilfully and effortlessly.

Mature generations of women who are managing and leading need
to find ways to become more visible more easily so they stand out
for all the right reasons. They need to claim the recognition they
deserve and to remain committed to their own career success.

CHAPTER 2

IT'S EVEN TOUGHER FOR EXECUTIVE WOMEN

Self-promotion can be tough for executive women ...

... we're damned if we do, yet doomed when we don't.

Research tells us that most of us aren't especially comfortable with it; even when we get it right there's likely to be someone in the wings ready to cut us down to size for being too loud, too quiet, too nice, too assertive, too lucky, too ambitious, not ambitious enough, too ... everything.

Unfortunately, the social penalty for getting it wrong is even worse and can make you wonder if it's worth doing it at all. This leads to a lack of confidence and hesitation about tactics that really work.

'Who does she think she is? (Argh!)

Never fear. All is not lost. Here are my three go-to questions that help you stand out and get noticed—for all the right reasons.

1   What do you stand for?
2.   Why is that important?
3.   How does it add value?

Once you are comfortable articulating all three, self-promotion becomes a breeze. And don't forget to get out of our own way first. It makes it so much easier.

Back yourself, sell yourself and articulate your expertise in language the business values and understands.

What helps you to self-promote more effectively?

Socialisation, stereotypes and bias: Gender, age, cultural

Recently, I spoke about self-promotion to a cohort of women for one of Australia's big four banks. It was part of a program to encourage and empower female talent within the business. These events are typically not limited to women, so it was encouraging to see a few men in the room (including one of the male business leaders as our host and champion). *When we only preach to the converted nothing changes.*

The male host opened the session by sharing that he also understood the challenges around self-promotion. He shared that he had struggled with confidence and self-promotion for much of his career. He wasn't naturally outgoing; it didn't come easily to him and he was far more comfortable not self-promoting. Everyone in the room identified with his story. He shared that while it had only impacted him, he was prepared to put up with the potential downside of not self-promoting, for example, being bypassed for plum assignments or results taken for granted or missing out on bigger salary increases.

He relayed that a big eye opener for him came when he reflected on his two very different children and how he could see that his more confident offspring was better at self-promoting than his less confident offspring. He noticed this was having a significant impact on the opportunities that were subsequently available for each of them even at this early stage in their working life.

The fact remained that while this male business leader acknowledged the detrimental impact of not self-promoting and of feeling and appearing less confident than his peers, this was the first time he understood that there was yet another link to gender—that most women do it even tougher in the self-promotion games.

The link between gender, confidence and self-promotion

There has been plenty of research into confidence and gender. Most of it concludes that women feel/are less confident. In my first book *Step Up, Speak Out, Take Charge,* I explored the idea that women express lower levels of confidence than men. There were a range of references to research and thinkers on the topic including authors of *The Confidence Code* (2014), Katty Kay and Claire Shipman. While there are multiple possible causes and contributors to women expressing and demonstrating lower levels of confidence (even scientists can't agree on whether it's nature or nurture), there is one contributor that remains the same, despite progress on many levels in the empowerment of women and girls, and that's the socialisation of women and girls being different to that of boys.

We encourage young boys to takes risk, to be adventurous, resilient and to have agency; whereas, we protect young girls. Stories and toys that, historically, were available for girls were more passive. Women's representation in movies, television and advertising is still skewed towards them playing 2nd fiddle or in more passive roles (despite what you might imagine). In fact, according to one study by San Diego State University, despite the appearance of many more movies with strong female leads, women accounted for only 24% of protagonists in the 100 top grossing domestic films of 2017—a decrease of 5% from the year before.

The impact of all of these things, and more, is that girls with fewer strong leadership female role models are *still* growing up to believe they have less agency and less of a sense of personal power, which leads to lower confidence. I love Elizabeth Gilbert's perspective:

> *'I was not rescued by a prince, I was the administrator of my own rescue'.*

Many women find they must become the administrator of their own rescue. A number of my clients are either the main or solo breadwinner in their family unit. These women, and many others, are not passively waiting around to be rescued, but are, in fact, forging strong career paths. Yet they still do it tough. The relatively new maxim 'you cannot be who you cannot see' makes it tough for women to see themselves in the top job. Additionally, when women do win the top role and are asked how they got there, they frequently comment that they were *in the right place at the right time*, or they were *lucky*. The socialised stereotype for women is not to display real effort and that being discovered is somehow better than making it happen. After all, men sweat and women dew in an idealised 1950s world. 'No effort required here.' 'I'm a natural.' All notions from a world where women wait. If we don't see many other women doing a particular activity, we assume, rightly or wrongly, that it's not necessarily something we should do. Both leadership and self-promotion definitely fall into that category.

Another contributor to low confidence would have to be exclusion practices (whether intentional or not) that ensure women don't feel seen, heard or valued. It's all well and good to invite women to the party, but if we don't create environments that welcome them, like including them in the conversation and enabling them to participate in decision making and valuing their contribution, then surely this contributes to lower levels of agency and confidence. It definitely takes a certain type of person to confidently pitch themselves in an area where they don't feel welcome. And while many leaders say they are focusing on culture rather than quotas and other mechanisms, to unpick and unpack exclusion tactics, I'm a big believer in the *Yes And* approach—where organisations focus on culture *and* quotas or other mechanisms, to ensure things change faster. After the change we can go back to purely focusing on culture to ensure the change sticks.

Does the mantra of low agency and low confidence become a self-fulfilling prophecy?

Women are far more likely to express that they don't feel bulletproof. After all, the socialisation of men and boys towards toughness and resilience doesn't naturally lend itself to expressing vulnerability. For many men, this is of particular concern as I'm sure it's quite stifling.

However, back to women, confidence and self-promotion ... whether you think you can, or think you can't, you are absolutely, categorically right (thanks Henry Ford). The risk to the individual is if they believe they're not as confident or that they can't self-promote as well as others, it will in fact become a self-fulfilling prophecy. If we're told continually that we are less confident, then will we become that way? If we are told we don't have as much agency, will this makes us have less agency? And if we are told it's hard to self-promote, then it will be hard to self-promote.

So for the remainder of the book (keeping in mind that our socialisation is telling us one thing), know that you can rewrite the story, not just for yourself, but for the women and men, and for girls and boys who come after you, so that we no longer feel that we walk a perilous knife edge between flying our own flag and flagrant self-promotion.

Social penalty and backlash

Inspired by a fabulous South African campaign turning stereotypes about women on their head.

I overheard this on a flight last week: 'She's a nag'. It turns out she (the nag) was the Chief Compliance Officer.

True story **#couldntmakeitup**

Me? Eye rolling with zero poker face ...

Love it!

Stereotypes used as a weapon against women

I love the South African advertising campaign mentioned above because it highlights how we use stereotypes to keep women in their place. The age-old chestnut of the hen pecked husband with the nagging wife is alive and well, and frequently, women in the workplace are tarred with that brush to keep them in their place.

Stereotypes are pretty powerful, aren't they? At times, they can be hurtful and harmful because it means we don't see the full person. Instead, we underestimate them or deliberately keep them in their place by labelling them. We use labels to keep women (in the workforce) in their place in a passive-aggressive way. This campaign drew attention to this. Then my fabulous LinkedIn network chipped in and give us a few more. Here is a range of labels frequently used against women when they were just doing their job:

- She's a nag because she works in compliance.
- She always needs her space because she's an architect.
- She likes to argue because she's a lawyer.

- She talks a lot because she's a professor.
- She wants to fix you because she's a GP.
- She only cares about your money because she's an accountant.
- The kids are her job because she's a paediatrician.
- She's a gold digger because she works in mining.

Beware the stereotyped assumptions in your workplace and call them out when you see or hear them.

The link between social penalty, gender, backlash and self-promotion

What do we mean by social penalty? When our peers and those around us (including women) punish us in some way socially, by ignoring, excluding, criticising, undermining or unfriending us.

There are several areas where social penalties are applied. Here are five that could potentially cause you to not want to call attention to yourself (ever again). In fact, because I don't want you to feel threatened or put off, I've deliberately kept them a little light.

1. **Who does she think she is?!:** When you do something that goes against the stereotype. The entire category of self-promotion fits here. Given the stereotyped norm is for women to wait until they are noticed, any self-promotion activity for anything other than naturally looking attractive runs the risk of social penalty.

2. **How dare she!:** When we do self-promote and we get it slightly wrong; maybe we're a bit overly enthusiastic, loud, brash, not subtle enough, too OTT.

3. **How unladylike, no wonder?!:** When we self-promote in a way that works for men, which is a subcategory of 1 and 2, but not

really. We affectionately forgive guys who we know are bragging, but we wouldn't do the same for a woman. The assumption is that a male leader is confident and a woman still has to jump through hoops to prove herself, so self-promoting just like a bloke definitely runs the risk of social penalty.

4. **Serves her right!:** When we self-promote and get it really wrong by being overtly salesy, pushy or assertive. Maybe we appear in the wrong magazines given our future goals, align ourselves with the wrong brands or are misquoted by the press.

5. **She deserves it!:** When you stand out due to scarcity but are in the wrong place at the wrong time, and where there is the need for a scapegoat—it's likely to be the woman. There is a concept of the Glass Cliff, where female leaders are brought in to fix a really big problem. If they fail, they become a scapegoat and this turns into a career limiting move.

Let me be clear, these things don't automatically happen to us when we self-promote. However, our own beliefs, biases and stereotyped assumptions kick into play, and it may just be that we're worried that we'll be tarred with these brushes. So the outcome is still the same whether or not we believe it—we don't self-promote, and we continue to perpetuate the cycle.

 Activity

Reflect on your recent self-promotion activities consider this:

What was I worried about? Did 'that' really happen? Or was it my imagination?

It's far easier for men

Remember the male leader in the bank who felt uncomfortable? While I don't want to diminish his concerns about it being tough for him, as it truly is a tough gig climbing the corporate ladder for anyone who is an introvert, even in his discomfort, he still has gender going for him. Why?

- Even as an introvert, he is not blamed with taking jobs away from other men. He is a man; therefore, he is eligible for a role. He is, in fact, a quiet achiever.
- Even if he becomes a bit brash, a bit of a braggart or over the top in any self-promotion activities, the backlash and potential for criticism is simply nowhere near as bad. After all, he is simply behaving as many men do.
- Even if he gets it wrong, he's more likely to be given another chance because 'boys will be boys!'
- Plus, there are far more men leading, standing out, sticking their head up above the crowd (so to speak), so he would not appear unusual—he is one of many.

The stereotype remains that men are able to self-promote; therefore, when he does it, it's expected and it's okay. Whereas when a woman self-promotes, stands out from the crowd or becomes more visible (unless it's in the realm of helping others or other more stereotypically feminine disciplines), she runs the risk of criticism, even if she does it well.

Backlash effect

While social penalty is one thing, the threat of backlash is an even stronger deterrent. This fear of backlash, whether real or imagined, plays a huge role in contributing to *leaning out* behaviours. It's called the *backlash effect*.

In *Disruptions in Women's Self-Promotion: The Backlash Avoidance Model* (2010), we learn that 'self-promoting women's fear of backlash inhibits activation of a goal-focused, locomotive regulatory mode, which subsequently interferes with self-promotion success'. Our fear of any potential backlash, including social penalty, gets in the way of our efforts with self-promotion activities. This same process does not impact men. There is a higher social penalty when women get it wrong. There is highly publicised criticism for women caught in the crossfire, by which we are horrified.

What do I mean by backlash?

- Criticised
- Ostracised
- Sacked
- Demoted
- Bullied at work
- Demonised at work
- Kept off plum assignments
- Hung out to dry and being made a scapegoat
- Trolled on social media
- Blamed or made to look incompetent by the media
- Made to look incompetent by the media for our femininity ...

... to just name a few.

The fear of these very real issues happening is alive and well. Many women I speak with are nervous of trolls—and rightly so. I choose LinkedIn to self-promote because I feel as though I have more control over my destiny with the ability to block, hide, report and delete any offensive comments or messages. I also feel as though the very nature of LinkedIn being linked to your workplace and peers, keeps the conversations more positive on the whole. But for those who find themselves in the public eye, the threat of backlash is real.

Case study

My particular interest in self-promotion, and the social penalty and potential for backlash was finely tuned in the wake of the Australian Royal Banking Commission's investigation into the performance of AMP in 2018. At the time, Catherine Brenner was chair of AMP. During the fallout of the report which demonstrated obvious unethical, illegal and systemic poor practices at AMP, Ms Brenner was criticised for her beauty regime, her appearance and how she 'networked' her way to the top rather than the job at hand. (What the?!)

What was concerning, but not surprising unfortunately, was that these journalists weren't all men. In fact, female journalists were some of the main contributors to this weirdly skewed criticism as though her femaleness was at fault rather than her leadership. They would not have criticised a man in the same way—and didn't. And what does a beauty regime have to do with her ability to chair anyway?

Had Ms Brenner not looked after herself, not networked and not self-promoted, she would have left herself open to criticism. To paraphrase General David Morrison, 'the double standards we walk past are the double standards we accept'. The double standards abound when it comes to women and self-promotion.

It definitely felt like a witch-hunt. My instinct tells me that executive and professional women throughout Australia were distressed by this witch-hunt, and it has had significant impact on the aspirations of a generation of young female potential leaders who will now think twice before self- promoting. This is the journalistic equivalent to trolling or bullying, and it needs to stop. Criticise the program, the policy, the process, the performance, but do not criticise the person—and certainly not her femaleness or femininity. Ms Brenner's situation is a classic example of damned when she did, yet doomed if she didn't.

The modesty effect and other research

What does a black box, that allegedly emits a subliminal noise in the middle of a room, have to do with women and career? More than you might imagine ...

Self-promotion can be tricky for executive women. We're damned if we do yet doomed if we don't.

The social penalty or backlash for getting it wrong can be harsh. The modesty norm remains strong for many and this puts many women off.

Enter science and a subliminal noise generator.

Researchers were looking for a way to distract participants (women) from their self-promotion self- consciousness. They created a task that required two groups of women to participate in a self- promotion activity. One group was put in a room where there was a distracting subliminal noise generator in their room ... they strangely performed far better in the activity.

The key? Not to go out and buy a generator because when a 3rd group was told about it and they underperformed. Good to know we're not that gullible.

But the good news? When yet another group was told to write or brag *about a peer*, they did a great job too ... without the generator. Science. Go figure?

What helps you get over your natural modesty so you can self-promote more effectively?

The modesty norm

*'There are still many causes worth sacrificing
for, so much history yet to be made.'*

—Michelle Obama

Women are far more prone to the effects of the *Modesty Norm*. In most cultures, it's deemed socially unacceptable for women to boast. In fact, she should be demure, downplay her contribution and achievement and make sure others get the credit. This *Modesty Norm* is part of yet another complex weave of socialised beliefs and biases that women take with them on their pathway to the board room.

Research tells us:

- Women are socialised from a young age to be modest or humble.
- When women advocate and promote on behalf of others, they are great at it (peer promotion is a tactic featured later in this book).
- The socialised *helper* archetype for women is incredibly strong and acceptable.
- As a society, we look more favourably on female leaders who nurture and support others. Hillary Clinton, on her Australian tour in 2018, spoke about her approval ratings before and after she stepped out onto her own platform. When she was supporting others, her approval ratings were high. When she was standing on her own platform, her ratings plummeted.

We are more likely to do things we don't like or are scared of including self-advocacy and self- promotion, when it's linked to a deeper sense of why. *Fear* researchers, who were looking at why some people are able to do terrifying things despite their fear, found that fire fighters, who were deeply connected to their sense of purpose, were able to face seemingly insurmountable challenges for the greater good. (Clark, 2011)

In a nutshell, just like in negotiation (which, I wrote about at length in *Step Up, Speak Out, Take Charge*), women know how to self-promote but hesitate because they are nervous of the social penalty or backlash when and if we get it wrong. The Catch-22 is that the less you do it, the less confident you are in the future. And the cycle continues.

Q. What depresses the modesty norm? A. When self-promotion activities are aligned to a cause. If there is a deeper sense of why, a purpose or a mechanism that helps you *escape the discomfort of defying the modesty norm,* you are not only far more likely to self-promote, but you are likely to achieve better outcomes.

As Jessi L. Smith and Meghan Huntoon, wrote in *Women's Bragging Rights: Overcoming Modesty Norms to Facilitate Women's Self-Promotion* (2013):

> Those who violated the modesty norm with a misattribution source reported increased interest, adopted fewer performance-avoidance goals, perceived their own work to be of higher quality, and produced higher quality work. Results suggest that when a situation helps women to escape the discomfort of defying the modesty norm, self-promotion motivation and performance improve.

However, it's not just women. There are some cultures where humility and modesty are deeply ingrained for men and women.

This insight is important to anyone who finds themselves in a situation struggling with modesty or humility and the need to self-promote. If you can dig deep and find your connection to a deeper sense of why, a sense of purpose, a mission, values, a theme that drives your career, or simply find a mechanism that helps you ignore your socialised modesty norm, you will find it far easier to self-promote, and perform.

Women criticising other women

I'm not keen on writing this section because I don't want to contribute to the myths, misinformation and misogyny that already exists for women with leadership aspirations. Rightly or wrongly, women have a reputation for criticising or penalising other women by being catty, bitchy or overtly negative towards their female peers or subordinates.

But is this really true? Is this perception encouraged simply as an exclusionary tactic, a diversionary blame game, or a way of keeping (other) women in their place? We need to know, so I've decided to air the topic, rather than hide from it. I hope to help you make up our own mind about how to react, behave or respond when you hear that women criticise other women, or when you find yourself in a situation where you are critiquing others for things other than objective performance measures or when you are feeling threatened by a more ambitious junior staffer who appears to be challenging you.

Queen Bee Syndrome

Historically, the traits valued in the rarefied air of the C-suite were assertiveness, combativeness and competitiveness, and the women who got to the top were *rewarded* for those *masculine* traits. Hence, *Queen Bee Syndrome* was born; whereby, some women made their way to the top, then deliberately held other women back.

The phrase was repurposed by a Dutch psychologist, Naomi Ellemers, who examined the lack of senior level women in academia. She had assumed that it was men keeping women out of senior roles. But what she discovered was the few women in senior roles were equally, if not more, exclusionary. Scarcity of opportunities drove even more competitive and assertive behaviours. The phrase stuck and it became an overused label when dealing with resistance towards women in power.

I suspect too that we've all had a female boss whom we remember as being tough as nails, harder on women than men, and certainly not one to be 'throwing back the net' let alone 'throwing down the ladder' for other talented women in the organisation.

But was her behaviour more memorable because:

- She was a female boss and still relatively unique?
- She was tough on other women because she didn't want to be seen as favouring them?
- She was simply unaware of the impact her behaviours and tactics had on her female staff because no-one had called her out on it?
- She was in survival mode, in a highly competitive, combative and assertive world where everyone was waiting for her to fail?
- Or a combination of any or all these factors?

Add into the mix the stereotype for women to be inclusive, collaborative and supportive. We hold our female boss to a higher standard than we might do her male peers; this a recipe for pejorative name calling even if there are elements of truth in it. The *stereotype effect* is a strong driver.

As Madeleine Albright famously said,

> *'There is a special place in hell for women who don't help other women.'*

We get it. I'm not excusing bullying tactics by any means. But sometimes people are caught in a cycle of stereotypes, expectations, limiting beliefs and fear that keeps them stuck behaving in ways that are distinctly unhelpful to other women and themselves. Studies have indicated that when professional women believe there's only room at the top for a few, they will bully and undermine their female colleagues and employees. Additionally, senior level women who champion younger women are more likely to get negative performance reviews—definitely a case of damned when you do, and another damned when you don't. (Johnson & Hekman, 2016)

No-one said it would be easy to get to the top, and once again, no-one was right.

Socialisation

The socialisation of women and girls is also frequently focused on outward appearance. I grew up being indoctrinated by *Dolly* magazine ... didn't you? And it's worse for young girls today. This can lead to comparing, judging, and critiquing, often from a perspective of not measuring up. The dark side of this is that in tearing others down, we feel we build ourselves up in some way. Yet the reverse is more likely to be true. The end result is that women who become more visible, find themselves more vulnerable, not just from attacks by men, but also other women.

Critiquing starts small

Recently, I participated on a magical, mystery bus tour with 20 other entrepreneurs. It was a heap of fun on a hot summer's day and we were all being deliberately pushed way out of our comfort zones with new people and new experiences. Many of my fellow passengers were smart, entrepreneurial women, possibly even more competitive by the very nature of their work.

On this tour, I experience an 'aha' moment. It was the end of a long, adventurous day and from the seat behind me, I heard two women beginning to critique other women on the sidewalk for their appearance.

I blew a mental gasket, then called out the behaviour.

Eleanor Roosevelt may have said, 'You wouldn't worry so much about what others think of you if you realised how seldom they do'. But perhaps she hadn't hung out in a bus with a group of women trying to stand out or compete with each other. Unfortunately, criticising others' appearance is not unusual and no-one sees it as a problem. For women in public life, the constant critiquing of their appearance, mannerisms and other personal attributes *is* a way of life, and this is from supporters, not necessarily trolls.

It's a socially acceptable habit in which we all indulge—a hobby. And I wonder what it will take for us to stop.

Why is this a problem?

- It's a temporary distraction. If women are busy criticising each other for seemingly trivial things, they aren't focused on where the action really is.
- It might temporarily make you feel good about yourself but long term, it damages your own confidence as you wonder

if others will be critiquing you when you take a stand or stand out for any reason.

- It causes unnecessary friction and slows things down. If you're serious about your career and taking it to the next level or you have an agenda you'd like to drive in your organisation, but you're side tracked by worries about what other people will think of you, you'll definitely take longer to launch.
- It can trigger shame. Women on the end of unnecessary criticism of a personal nature often feel embarrassment, guilt or shame.

When we criticise others or hold others back, we are damaging ourselves and undermining our own efforts to stand out from the crowd and be noticed. Let's stop with the criticising and competitiveness with other women and simply get on with the business of creating work environments that support and champion the endeavours, perspectives and unique talents of everyone.

Losing likeability and the *angry woman* stigma

Are we back in the 1950s?

I was recently shocked by a sexist comment. '**#Women** simply can't manage money as well as men. Women don't care about money, they care about people,' he said.

This wasn't just any sexist guy, it was a **#Financial** columnist for a well-known publication. WTF?!? I nearly had an apoplexy! What an insult to most of the women in my circle of acquaintance, if not all women everywhere.

I can't even excuse his age because my grandma (even older than he) was AWESOME at **#financialmanagement.** But bias and stereotypes are rampant in our business world. With so few women visibly leading the financial space … it's no wonder.

It's far easier to accept the old narrative and stereotyped norms as a version of the truth. Hang out with enough people who think the same as you, and you'll end up with a bad case of confirmation bias to boot.

Here are three well-known financially savvy women:

Sally Krawcheck, Ellevest
Christine Lagarde, IMF (and closer to home)
Gail Kelly, 1st female CEO of a major Aussie bank

Let's kick this stereotype to the kerb (yet again).

The above comments were made during a conversation between me (executive coach for career- minded women) and a man (financial columnist) who sat next to me on a flight to Brisbane. When the conversation ended, I felt frustrated, flabbergasted … and angry. Oh no. I'm 'that' angry woman!

I wanted to address the issue on the spot but I was too riled up. I wanted to tell people but I was flying in a tiny tin tube 30,000 feet above the earth. And I am also socialised enough to know that female anger doesn't always further a cause and can be used against her. So instead, I did everything in my power to turn that rage into something positive, so I wouldn't end up suffering negative consequences. Here's what I did:

1. I immediately drafted a blog to capture my rage.

2. I sought a 3rd person perspective on my draft to ensure I was expressing my views effectively and that my message would drive change.

3. I sent a copy of *Don't get angry, get even* to all the financially savvy women in my feed.

Why did I do all this? Because I, too, am extremely wary of being tarred with the *angry woman* stereotype because life is even tougher for angry women.

The angry woman stereotype

The stereotype of an angry woman is a negative one; it's suggests they are emotional, out of control, less logical and less than credible. Words and labels used to describe angry women include bitchy, witchy and hostile; whereas when men are perceived as angry, they are seen as strong and commanding.

> '*The phenomenon of female anger has often been turned against itself, the figure of the angry woman reframed as threat — not the one who has been harmed, but the one bent on harming.*'
>
> —Leslie Jamison, Jan 2018 New York Times

We all witnessed how US Senator Hillary Clinton was portrayed by the media when she displayed anger. It's a tough gig to remain credible as a woman when you are known for being angry. Clinton's moments of outrage contributed to derailing her campaign because women were equally as critical of her, as the men.

What the research says

Researchers from Arizona State University and the University of Illinois at Chicago looked at the differences in how we perceive angry men or women and highlighted the double standard.

They found that:

women's anger worked against them, while men's anger served as a 'powerful' tool of persuasion. When the holdout was a male who expressed anger, participants significantly doubted their own opinion, even when they were in the majority. But if the holdout was a woman who expressed anger, she actually had less influence over participants — so much so, that it was the only scenario in the study in which participants became more confident in their own opinion that opposed that of the woman'.

Angry women are perceived as violating the socialised norm, which leads to further social penalty.

The alternatives for women are pretty limited—grace and poise under pressure still come to mind. Nice is another option. yet we all know that 'nice girls' don't get the corner office.

Then that's it. Nada.

Nice as a subset

In 2018, I ran a series of events around Nice Girl Leadership to explore the issues surrounding leading as a female, and in particular, being nice and likeable. The following key points were emphasised by women in the audience:

- Nice is not naïve.
- Nice does not mean being compliant, complicit or even capitulating.
- Nice doesn't preclude being direct, assertive or highly competitive.
- Nice can mean being willing to have tough conversations or using tough love principles to help someone move forward.

- Nice means being kind and gracious; graciousness goes a long way in business and is hugely underestimated.
- Nice and likeable aren't necessarily the same and definitely not to be confused with needing to be liked.

Helen Mandziejewski, an inspired attendee, emailed me after one of the events:

'Being nice means being true to yourself and the situation by setting appropriate boundaries without aggression, anger, hatred or resentment. It's about being strong and steadfast in your convictions whilst opening your heart to show kindness, compassion and gentleness towards others'.

When we self-promote, we open ourselves up to public scrutiny from others. In order to remain effective, in control of the narrative and focused on achieving our end goal, it's incredibly helpful to know who we are and how we fit into the big picture with regard to the various aspects of socialisation, stereotype and bias in advance so they don't derail us in the future. Those who are comfortable in their own skin and who have done the work in advance will self-promote far more effectively.

CHAPTER 3

THE BUSINESS CASE FOR SELF-PROMOTION

Should you ask for a #raise?

Does anyone remember in 2014, when Nadella, the **#Microsoft** CEO advised 'that women who have **#goodkarma** don't need to ask for a raise—they should get one naturally'?

(GASP! 😱)

He has publicly apologised many times and now gives completely different advice.

Research doesn't reflect the idea of women being recognised for their work and given raises accordingly. Instead, studies and statistics regularly point to systemic bias affecting women's career paths. Across tech, women are offered 4% less on average than men for the same role in the same company. A 2017 study conducted by LeanIn and McKinsey & Co indicates that, when women do ask for a raise, they are seen as 'bossy' or 'aggressive'.

Despite this, a study by Artz, Goodall, and Oswald (2018) suggests that women actually do ask for raises as often as men, but only receive raises 15% of the time. Men receive them 20% of the time.

So what is Nadella's recent advice? Women should

1. Advocate for themselves
2. Find other allies, male or female, who can advocate for them.

3. And 'make sure that they don't accept status quo.'

What's your best advice for winning a raise?

What can we learn about self-promotion from the rise of the celebrity CEO and the cult of celebrity?

Entrepreneurial CEOs and executives are curating and developing their own reputation and brand on and offline, which is delivering better business outcomes. It helps build awareness; it's cheaper than advertising; and it's proactive, rather than reactive by getting on the front foot with messaging and taking charge of the narrative.

'Crafting a brand strategy for yourself as the face of your company is arguably as important as developing your company's brand image'.

—Brant Pinvidic, Forbes

In Australia, we can learn from these three female leaders with celebrity status:

- Naomi Simson, Founding Director, Red Balloon Days and more recently remembered for her role on Shark Tank.
- Janine Allis, Founder of Boost Juice, part owner of Retail Zoo and she also featured on Shark Tank.
- Melanie Perkins, co-founder and CEO of Canva and LinkedIn star.

This is important for a range of reasons:

- In a world where self-promotion is the new black, younger generations are used to branding, and thinking of themselves and their lives as a saleable commodity.
- We're in an era demanding trust and transparency.
- Consumers trust individuals more than institutions.
- *Reputation* was identified in the top four concerns for CEOs (KPMG, 2018).
- More than 45% of a company's reputation is linked to that of the CEO (Weber Shandwick, 2015).

While these points all refer to celebrity or CEO status, the lessons for those who are serious about their career remain.

- Executive branding and self-promotion have never been more important.
- People, including staff, want to follow ideas and inspiration that moves them.
- Authenticity is critical; not only does it make it easier for you, but audiences and others see straight through a fake persona.
- You can provide more value by being a 'micro celebrity' than hiding behind the organisation or division you lead.
- It's not a waste of time. It's the cost of doing business in a modern, digital, globalised and increasingly complex environment, where people are looking for clarity and certainty, and to follow those with whom they identify and trust.

Do executive women need to self-promote more?

One of the biggest fears for the senior women with whom I work is that they simply don't feel seen, heard or valued. They've arrived at a point in their careers where the competition is tighter (fewer senior roles), where they are often the only woman in the team, and where they appear to have lost traction. They feel as though their contribution is dismissed or taken for granted. This leaves them feeling used. Plum assignments or sexy opportunities are more easily distributed to younger talent in other divisions or other men on the team.

These women are on constant alert for others taking credit for their work. Is this being hyper sensitive? No. In three recent client cases, each woman had experienced at least one incident of a peer taking credit for their work, including repurposing presentations without attribution and taking the glory with blatant disregard (aka lying) for contribution that wasn't theirs. In another instance, a client was simply marginalised by peers after she had done all the work on a collaborative project.

When women do get the credit, the rewards or recognition aren't there in the same way as they are for male peers. Promotions are not as easily landed and equal pay offers simply don't eventuate (despite this being illegal). I'm currently working with two women who have discovered they are being paid between $100K and $220K less than male peers. Yes, they're angry, frustrated and working for restitution.

'I would venture to guess that Anon, who wrote so many poems without signing them, was often a woman.'

—Virginia Woolf

(Sidenote on a balanced voice: *I do my own part to even up the score on balanced voice by spending extra time and effort to quote women in the first instance where possible.*)

I would venture to guess that there are many business initiatives that wouldn't have happened without a woman's contribution, yet the success has been claimed or attributed to a man. This overlooking of women's contribution is not new. Throughout history, we have seen multiple examples of women's contribution either missed or downplayed by others. Famously, Madam Curie's contributions to science were initially ignored by the Nobel Prize nominating committee. No recognition of Marie's contributions was offered, nor was there any mention of her name in the award. After petitioning by others including her husband and a sympathetic committee member, the award was modified and she is now acknowledged as a Nobel Prize Winner.

The super successful women in my circle of acquaintance are the women who have fought tooth and nail for recognition of their contribution. This frequently meant getting out of their own way, self- promoting, backing themselves and self-advocating for themselves and their cause until they didn't feel uncomfortable any more or their contribution was recognised. Why? Because they knew their value and they knew that it was the right thing to do.

Lack of sponsored networks among senior level peers inside industry or organisations would be another reason women need to self-promote more. Without these informal structures with peer-to-peer support and advocacy, self-promotion becomes even more critical. If more self-promotion is truly not possible for you, then it's imperative that you self-promote smarter, ensuring everything you do delivers bang for its buck in terms of your career advancement and recognition. This means smart strategies need to remain forefront of mind throughout your career.

You can't afford the following without having smart self-promotion strategies in place (to put it simply, you'll struggle to be recognised when you do lift your head back up):

- To bury yourself inside a project for a couple of months (becoming invisible).
- To take an overseas secondment for a few years (or more) without focusing on maintaining your networks back home.
- To take career breaks without maintaining connections back in your career world.

The easy path for organisations is to notice and recognise those they already know, those they can see and those they feel will be around long term. So self-promotion is critical, and yes, you'll likely need to self-promote more and smarter to overcome those blocks.

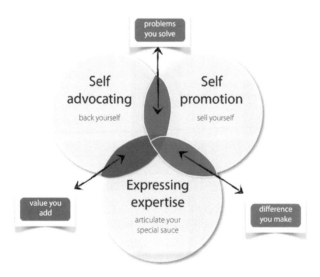

Figure 1: Self-promotion unpacked

Developing competence and confidence around backing yourself, selling yourself and/or ideas, and expressing your expertise in language the business understands and values, should be part and parcel of your professional development. As with any new skill, it takes practice, so don't wait too long to start. It is a murkier area if you are a woman learning to self-promote. But you still need to do it to ensure you win the next raise or promotion more easily; your voice is heard within the business; and you make a bigger difference far more easily.

From invisible to invincible and beyond

**I used to be a wallflower, always shy and retiring,
and I wouldn't say boo to a goose.**

I would worry about a lot: that I'd be wrong, I wasn't perfect, that people wouldn't like me or what I said, or that I'd get 'found out'.

This left me in the zone of waiting to be discovered, waiting to be noticed, waiting till I felt better prepared and waiting for the time to be right.

Then something happened. I started working with a coach and identified that I needed to let go of many things and none of them were my professional expertise. I subsequently let go of:

- the need to do everything
- the need to be liked
- the need to be perfect
- the need to know everything
- the need to be right
- the need to be in control.

When I let go of 'the need', all of a sudden, articulating my perspective, sharing my results and expressing my opinion became a doddle.

I know I'm not alone in this. Every day I speak to four or five women who share a similar story and experience. These are super smart executives who are nervous of expressing their opinion in a public forum.

When we operate in the realm of waiting for the planets to align, it's always going to be a tough gig. There will never be a good time. Self-promotion becomes much easier when you follow this prescription:

- What are you passionate about? Find your passion.
- Why are you doing this? Find your sense of purpose.
- Where will you get the best bang for your buck? Find a platform that works for you.

And the right time, while rarely perfect, is now.

What helps you self-promote more effectively? To take a stand, to express your opinion or to talk about your results?

#business
#career
#womenofimpact

What do I mean by invisible?

Hidden, not easily seen, heard or valued. I don't need to define invisible to you because you've probably felt it at some stage in your career. Invisible means you are overlooked, bypassed. You can be in the same meeting room as everyone else, but you rarely contribute because no-one listens when you say anything.

You're never at networking functions and if you did go, you remain in the background. You hate taking a spot in the limelight because it's not your place—others deserve it more.

And what is invincible?

Invincible is the feeling of being in control of your own destiny. Other people know exactly who you are, what you stand for, and why it's important to you. You are offered more opportunities, your presence and opinion are sought out, your contribution is valued, recognised and remunerated. Invincible doesn't mean bulletproof; however, it does mean you are futureproofed, resilient and able to find something new far more easily. As a result of feeling invincible, you're not only first on the invitation list, you're afforded the benefit of any doubt, and given a second chance when things go wrong. The cape of invincibility is embedded with feminine leadership superpowers that help you self-promote and win more effectively, so you can throw down the net and bring others with you without feeling threatened.

IMPACT	EXECUTIVE BRAND	FOCUS	
Invincible	Rockstar	National / Global recognition	Empowered
Incredible	Dynamo	Highly sought after	Empowered
Indispensable	Fixer	Solving complex problems	
Inconsequential	Enabler	Makes other people look good	Disempowered
Insubstantial	Player	At the opening of an envelope	Disempowered
Invisible	Workhorse	Relentless execution	

Figure 2: From Invisible to Invincible executive branding

The model above is a diagnostic tool to help you reflect on your brand and the impact you are having inside your organisation. It is also a road map of where to go next. Start at the bottom and work your way up to discover with which category you identify most.

The Workhorse

Focus: Relentless execution.

Benefits: Volume of work and being able to push the proverbial uphill.

Theme: Invisible.

Negative: Being noticed for doing hard work all the time will keep you stuck in a rut of playing small.

Description: Usually, the Workhorse is someone with a strong work ethic who believes in getting the job done. This position is often accompanied by comments such as 'give a busy person something to do and they'll get it done' or 'she's got her nose to the grindstone'. Many women find themselves stuck in this rut. They are highly conscientious and have a high volume workload as they juggle work and family obligations and try to keep everyone happy. The expectations of women are higher so cutting corners comes at a social cost. The Workhorse simply cannot see the wood for the trees with only enough energy to get to the goal post, rather than think creatively and innovatively.

Additionally, the Workhorse's skill set has become fine-tuned in delivering at high volume or a fast pace, rather than expanding the skill set or going deeper into a specialist niche. This leaves the individual exhausted. Typically, many Workhorse tasks can be outsourced or delegated, which leaves the Workhorse in a vulnerable position with potentially outdated skills. The Workhorse suffers bouts of exhaustion; they wonder if it's all worthwhile and frequently lean out after not receiving the recognition they deserve. A team of Workhorse staff won't question, challenge or innovate easily. They'll come in, do the job and do it well, then leave without necessarily thinking outside the square.

The fix: Find, implement and talk about ways to work smarter. Take time to look up and ask yourself *Is this the smartest way I can deliver this? Is there another way? Is there a better* way?

The Player

Focus: Being seen, heard and frequently said to be the one who is 'at the opening of an envelope'.

Benefits: Great networker with high visibility and a seat at the table.

Theme: Inconsequential/insubstantial**.**

Negative: Not necessarily valued. Imposter Syndrome, as you wonder why you're in the room, and .... after a while, other people are left wondering why you are there too.

Description: There is saying 'you never get a second chance to make a first impression'. While we know about the *Halo effect* (where people remember a good first impression far longer than you imagine), this statement has an element of truism—true but not really. At some level, if you can't back up your presence, your seat at the table or your opinion, then you'll be considered a lightweight and run the risk of damaging your reputation.

We all know the Player. They are a strong networker, they look smart or stylish, they know how to meet and greet and are often an extrovert. They're in the right place at the right time; however, no-one really knows what they stand for and down the track their entire presence will be in question. A Player on LinkedIn, for example, is nervous of expressing their true opinion, but are trying to network, so they *Like* and *Comment* 'great article' constantly. The Player in the boardroom is the person who passes off their perspective by responding with 'what she/he said'. Younger women often tell me they are pigeonholed as a Player: nice to have in the room to meet quotas or targets but no-one really thinks they have any substance or value to add.

The fix: Take a position. Work out what you stand for, why it's important and how it impacts or adds value. Then learn to articulate that in different ways and on different forums so you don't sound like a broken record. This way, you'll leave a lasting impression, one with substance, not as a lightweight and this will guarantee you an invitation back.

The Enabler

Focus: Great at making other people look good.

Benefits: Supportive, great 2IC and other people love them so they keep them there.

Theme: Invaluable.

Negative: Doesn't like taking credit or ownership; therefore, is perceived to lack accountability or agency.

Description: Have you ever seen that meme from the 90s, 'oh no, I must have left my baby at the supermarket'? The Enabler is about to have one of those days. They run the risk of waking up one day and realising they've spent all their career making everyone else look good, but they *forgot* to do the same for themselves.

However, the Enabler or helper archetype is strong for many women as we're socialised to help others. In fact, women are put on pedestals for helping others—Michelle Obama in her role as First Wife. The stereotype around this supporting role for women is so strong, that those who do stand out, run the risk of social criticism. Hilary Clinton, in her 2018 Australian Tour commented on likability for women.

Among the comments, she highlighted that women who get ahead on a platform of being 'in service' and supporting others, don't lose in likability. But women who try and emerge from that supportive enabler role, leave themselves open to criticism, rightly or wrongly.

 Case study

Mary was a highly successful corporate leader known for her servant leadership style. She was incredibly supportive of her team. In return, her team loved her and bent over backward to achieve KPIs and deliver above and beyond. Mary's department was kicking huge goals, and Mary was seen as a huge asset to the business. Then came a leadership change. A new male CEO was appointed. He didn't see the value in servant leadership and Mary's enabler style. He appreciated that the team was delivering, but failed to see that if Mary wasn't there supporting, helping, cheering them along and clearing roadblocks, they wouldn't deliver. In Mary's next performance appraisal, she was told to start kicking goals in her own right, or there would need to be performance discussions. Sad but true.

The fix: There is an expression from the real estate world, 'you cannot sell a secret'. Practice stepping out from the background every now and then. Find a platform on which you can take a stand, where you've got something to add and are comfortable standing alone. Then tell people about it.

The Fixer

Focus: Solves complex problems.

Benefits: Awesome at their role blending strategy, operations, wisdom of experience, emotional intelligence and deep subject matter expertise.

Theme: Indispensable.

Negative: You're kept in the role because organisations need more fixers. Anecdotally, being a Fixer works for men but not women. Men get promoted.

Description: You know you are a deep subject matter expert. You've been around the block; you know how your organisation and industry works; and you know yourself pretty well. You're great at solving complex and sometimes ambiguous problems. You know how to balance operational and strategic imperatives. You're good at nuance and emotional intelligence, and you do the stuff others can't. In fact, you know where all the *dead bodies* are because you hid them.

You imagine you're going to win a raise, a promotion or some meaningful recognition that leads to a better opportunity in the not too distant future. But all you get is 'thanks' and another messy, big, complex problem to solve. Don't get me wrong, we're all in the business of solving problems. For many of us, that's our role. However, you also need to self-promote, stand out, and receive reward and recognition for those solutions.

Interestingly, a male Fixer seems to get promoted, while a female Fixer is kept in place because they keep the machinery running.

The risk: While you're preoccupied with taking responsibility for and solving this complex problem, someone who is more comfortable with self-promotion (possibly a Player) will overtake you on the career ladder.

The fix: Learn to self-promote. Have a visibility plan in place. Schedule in regular time to network so that others also know of the value of your work and the outcomes you are in the process of delivering. Don't wait until the end of the big messy problem. Give progress reports.

 Case study

Cathy was a senior level technology and program leader. She knew her stuff. She had a large team kicking goals for an overseas client, and she had rave reviews from her team and her client. In fact, the client loved her so much, they've invited her to relocate. For whatever reason, Cathy wasn't in a position to do that, so she managed the time differences, from Australia, with some flexibility combined with late night stints and technology solutions.

The time difference and external client focus meant she had low visibility and a low profile within her organisation. Unfortunately, a couple of more politically astute (yet misguided) male peers tried to take advantage of this and marginalised her from meetings and opportunities. They even tried undermining her authority with her staff.

In response, Cathy became far more strategic when sharing news about her and her team's wins in public view. She also ensured she was visible at the right times with key decision makers. Given the time difference, she would start late at the office but went straight to the level with most of the leadership team to have formal and informal discussions—to be seen and heard by all the right people. She also ensured she got face time with her team on a regular basis, that they saw her, spoke with her. By doing this, she had the opportunity to share insights she'd gleaned from the leadership team.

This was a turnaround for Cathy, and after six months of focussing on being seen in the right place at the right time, with the right key messages, and ensuring she called out the poor behaviour of her peers, she is now achieving in a much bigger role, and she has landed a seat at the table.

That (imaginary) dotted line between The Fixer and The Dynamo

This line represents a significant change in mindset and accountability. Everything below the line represents *my career happens to me*. My career; my success; my reality are not really in my own control. I don't have agency over these things. While above the line represents *I create my own destiny*. It's up to me; the buck stops with me; I create my own reality, destiny, career success.

So are you ready to step over the dotted line?

The Dynamo

Focus: Getting out of your own way and speaking to your results. Feel the fear and self-promote anyway.

Benefit: In demand as a subject matter expert or advisor for exciting projects, opportunities.

Theme: Incredible.

The Dynamo has done the hard yards. They've worked their way through the ranks and understand the need for balance between getting things done and telling people about the benefits of getting things done. After all, great leadership is more than 50% bringing people along for the journey; therefore, inspiring others and selling them the value of the impact or benefit are all part and parcel of the role.

This person is comfortable with self-advocacy; they know what they stand for and can communicate this with skill and ease. They know how to take a position and regularly do so. The Dynamo is regularly invited to speak on panels and at conferences and advisory committees and boards. Their expert opinion and sage counsel is valued and respected. They know this doesn't happen by accident so the Dynamo collects evidence of wins and achievements and shares regularly. They reflect upon what it is they know and how it adds value. They have a plan (linked to their long- term career strategy) around how to communicate ideas, perspectives, wins and achievements to the broader community (speaking, publishing, interviews, LinkedIn, meetings, committees and panels). They also know how to speak of their results in a way that takes ownership but not credit, where credit was not due.

The risk: Professional jealousy by those left behind as the Dynamo is no longer seen around the office. They are perceived to be on junkets and not doing the work; therefore, slip back to Player status.

The fix: Continue to maintain your visibility with decision makers, stakeholders and key players. At this time more than ever, it's important for them to know what you are working on and how it's adding value.

The Rockstar

Focus: Global/national recognition.

Benefit: Boards, awards and accolades well beyond the walls of the organisation, which ensures your career is futureproofed to some degree. The Rockstar isn't smashing guitars, they are smashing perception, bias and glass ceilings.

Theme: Invincible.

The Rockstar is not only highly sought after but has achieved the corporate equivalent of Rockstar status that comes with global recognition. Boards, awards and accolades. The Rockstar has not only done the hard yards but has actively sought out opportunities to stand out, demonstrate thought leadership, take the conversation to the next level and fly the flag for themselves, their organisations or other causes more broadly.

They have a blend of promoting for the cause but not playing second fiddle, taking credit where credit is due but throwing back the net and bringing others along with them.

The Rockstar is not threatened by new players, different thinking or challenging ideas. The Rockstar relishes this new phase in their career as they thrive on challenge, being at the forefront and tackling new ideas.

The Rockstar executive understands how to tap into and harness the power of the cult of celebrity as both a customer and talent acquisition strategy along with retaining loyal staff and customers. They are able to harness that power with a strong online and offline presence, and demonstrate persuasive language and communication skills. After all, the Rockstar is in the business of creating a following that will benefit the brand or organisation they work for, and for themselves.

The risk: The Rockstar may feel invincible but that doesn't mean they are bulletproof. The cult of celebrity is seductive but the Rockstar must build in checks and balances. This includes regular feedback so they don't begin to believe their own hype, which can have serious implications where their own brand takes a departure from their own values or the strategic goals of the organisation. Additionally, with Tall Poppy Syndrome alive and well in Australia, (where we criticise those who dare to raise their head above the crowd) the Rockstar must ensure they know how to speak to their results but ensure that their results are backed up with quantifiable and qualifiable evidence, which goes a long way towards mitigating Imposter Syndrome as well as defending against external critics. A significant benefit of being a Rockstar executive, however, is the futureproofing nature of the broader business community knowing of your results. This is your insurance policy. If you do end up being cut down to size, it's far easier for you to quickly and successfully, re-establish yourself elsewhere.

Misconceptions about self-promotion

Every week, I speak with 20 or so women about self-promotion, how it helps their career and how it helps them deliver meaningful work outcomes. Missed out on a plum assignment? Maybe it's because you forgot to self-promote as much as your peer who ended up winning it.

Here are seven of the most common excuses or misconceptions that I hear around self-promoting:

1. *I just need to do great work.* Remember the famous 'build it and they will come' line from Kevin Costner's *Field of Dreams?* He built a baseball stadium and people magically turned up simply because it was there. In a highly competitive job market, where we confuse confidence with competence, you simply cannot afford to assume that people will see the value or commercial application of your experience or expertise. Additionally, algorithms, short attention spans and rapidly changing technologies rule the world. It's hard to sell a secret, so you'll need to do far more than create a program, post on LinkedIn, or just do great work. You need to sell the value of the great work you do—ergo you need to self- promote.

2. *My results should speak for themselves.* This is the most common expression I hear from busy executives who are beginning their self-promotion journey. Nearly everyone has this inner mental script, 'It's not fair. I shouldn't have to tell my boss how well I did. They should see for themselves; it's their job to manage me. My results should speak for themselves anyway'. Success will belong to those who can speak to their own results

without sounding like they're bragging. Ironically, success comes more easily to those who *do* brag than to those who don't speak at all. So start practicing now.

3. *When I land a new role, I don't need to self-promote any more.* This is another common misconception. Ambitious and successful women know this. They self-promote even when they start a new role. In fact, even more so. They remain visible inside and outside the business. They change the balance towards heavier internal self-promotion to help them fast-track their success in the first six months, and lighter external self-promotion to ensure people outside the organisation remember them. There is nothing worse than being buried in everything new with no room to do much more than survive, only to emerge after your first six months and find out people have forgotten you. People are fickle, attention spans are short, and there is always someone hungrier. Stay visible people. Stay visible.

4. *I don't really need the credit or recognition.* A common excuse after someone has missed out on a pay rise or promotion. But, yes you do. It's the currency of the organisation in which you work. If you don't value yourself enough to claim credit, others won't either, and someone else may just take credit on your behalf. It's a sign of healthy self-respect to claim credit where credit is due. If you don't respect yourself, others will also take you for granted. Once again, start practising now.

5. *I have to do this on my own.* Peer promotion is a great addition to your self-promotion toolkit. It really works for women because it doesn't trigger reactions about socialised stereotype biases. It's great to have others on your side who can fly the flag for 'brand you', reinforce your opinion and remind others how great you are.

It's far easier for me to say out loud that 'Michelle is a Rockstar'. It's far harder for me to say that about myself. So build a team of peers who are interested in career advancement but not interested in competing with you. Then help them to help you by providing them with evidence of your results and examples of what you do. Ask for references on LinkedIn, ask for positive feedback about your leadership brand. Your peers or others may just help you achieve Rockstar status without you having to sweat it out.

6. *I've got great sponsors/mentors/champions, so I'll be okay.* I've written about this frequently. I see many women who've hit a certain spot in their career without having to self-promote because they didn't have to by way of having been fast-tracked or because they had others smooth their way for them. Then when the time comes, they don't know how and it feels incredibly hard.

Do whatever you can do ensure you have the backing of great sponsors, mentors, champions and peers who support you. But if these people resign, retire or are made redundant, you will be left hanging out to dry with no self-promotion muscle, because you've never had to do it for yourself. You need to develop your own self-promotion skills (in addition to having great sponsors mentors and champions) so you can carve out your own career path.

As leadership expert, Avril Henry wisely says, *'No-one is as interested in your career as you are. So do something about it!'*

We imagine it's *all about me*. In fact, the most powerful self-promotion is rarely *all about me* and is far more outwardly focused. Remember the line from ABC's Kath and Kim, *'Look at moi'?* Unskilful self-promoters, whom we all try and avoid, make it all about them. Boring. And quite challenging. When we make it about the self, it's far more likely we'll become self-conscious or worried we'll appear self-absorbed or self-centred.

Instead when you take the *self* out of *self-* promotion and make it all about the problems you solve, the difference you make and the value you add, you'll do far better. Take it one step further and make sure this is in service to others—you'll be self-promoting like a Rockstar in no time.

More whys

So far, we've addressed the issues that get in the way for executive women who self-promote. What we've missed, however, is why they need to self-promote in the first place. Why self-promote at all? It feels uncomfortable and it can go wrong quite easily, so why bother?

In summary:

- It's a chance to showcase your unique interests or expertise.
- It's a chance to demonstrate or articulate the value of your expertise.
- It can ensure you get noticed by decision makers.
- You gain recognition and respect for your contribution.
- It can ensure you receive regular pay rises.
- It can help you futureproof your career by ensuring people inside and outside of your immediate department or organisation know how you add value (or perhaps know about your future goals and ambitions).
- It helps others know your long-term career goals (potentially keeping you in mind for future opportunities).
- It's great for team morale when others see their boss was acknowledged more broadly.
- It helps you make a far bigger difference in your chosen field.

If you still can't self-promote on your own behalf, you must do it on behalf of your staff. Self- promoting on behalf of the team helps others see the value of the business function you and your team delivers. Why is this important? As a people leader or manager, if you fall into the *too quiet, non self-promotional trap*, your department may miss out on budget during reshuffles or when pitching for budget during the regular budget cycle. The importance of the work you do will be underestimated and the work of your division potentially undermined. Not self-promoting can have far reaching negative effects like redundancies or staff losing motivation because the team isn't recognised. And while you may feel this isn't strictly self-promotion, self-promotion will be one of the tools you'll need to ensure your division is seen, heard, valued and in for the long haul.

 Activity

Rank yourself as a Workhorse, Player, Enabler, Fixer, Dynamo or Rockstar. Which category do you tend to operate in most? Which category would you like to spend more time in? Where would you like to go?

Think about what you might do differently. Pay attention to any beliefs, biases or baggage that come up for you when you think about standing out from the crowd. Journal, make lists, put plans in place for how you will tackle any internal resistance (your own beliefs, biases and baggage), which in turn will help you tackle that from others.

PART 2

CHAPTER 4

EIGHT VITAL COMPONENTS TO SUBTLY POWERFUL SELF-PROMOTION

Part 2 is an opportunity for you to do some work and rate yourself as you go. If you are going to get out of your comfort zone and self-promote more skilfully, then you must first understand the basic building blocks.

There are eight elements listed throughout this chapter where I invite you to rate yourself on a scale of 1–10 as to your current comfort, skill or progress with each element. (1 is low, 10 is high. You are not allowed to pick 7 because that's sitting on the fence.) The areas where you ranked yourself on the lower end will become your road map to explore on your self-promotion journey.

These elements are not self-promotion tactics per se, but rather some of the thinking work and preparation that will help you self-promote more easily.

1. Conduct a monthly mindset audit

Being good at self-promotion is a mindset game. If you fear self-promotion or the judgments others make, then your leadership journey is going to be far tougher. As you've learned so far, self-promotion can be a minefield. It is more easily navigated when you master various aspects of your mindset.

Growth mindset

> *'We like to think of our champions and idols as superheroes who were born different from us. We don't like to think of them as relatively ordinary people who made themselves extraordinary.'*
>
> —Carol S. Dweck

Have you heard about Carol Dweck's growth mindset? Carol is a Professor from Stanford University who coined the terms *fixed* and *growth mindset*. Her book *Mindset: Changing the Way You think to Fulfil Your Potential* (2017) is a must read, especially for any parents reading this.

- A fixed mindset is when you believe your abilities, talents and IQ are capped in some way. This limits your view of your own potential and what's possible for you. It stops you trying when you hit the cap of your current capability.
- A growth mindset is when you believe your abilities, talents and IQ can grow—you just need to keep trying.

Given the ambiguity and complexity around self-promotion, adopting a growth mindset is critical as you will need to deal with getting it wrong, not being good at it (initially), feeling like a fool and it feeling like a chore.

Possibility mindset

In my first book *Step Up, Speak Out, Take Charge*, I introduced the concept of a *Possibility Mindset*. It is bias towards optimism or a glass half full attitude. (Although my personal opinion is that those who are successful in this world are those who've already drunk the glass dry while everyone else is still debating whether it's half full or half empty.)

Those with a Possibility Mindset, will say 'heck yes' then puzzle out how to do it later. They fly by the seat of their pants and colour outside the lines. Importantly, they opt in, not out, as a default.

Research tells us that as women we have a tendency to self-select out way too soon. Instead of saying 'heck yes', we say 'no I'm not ready yet, I need to do more work'. Research also tells us that we express lower levels of confidence; we downplay our achievements and abilities and even underestimate ourselves. This has a significant impact on how we tackle stretch opportunities (The Institute of Leadership & Management).

A complete overhaul of mindset is required for your leadership and self-promotion journey, and monthly checks to ensure you haven't slipped back into bad habits are mandatory. I encourage executive women to think like champions, to opt in, not out and to regularly get out of their comfort zone. This is all much easier if they focus on three critical elements:

- The problems they get to solve.
- The difference they get to make.
- The value they get to add.

Activity

Rank your mindset management on a scale of 1–10 when it comes to self-promotion, and remember, you are not allowed to pick 7.

2. You have systems in place to proactively manage your beliefs, biases and baggage

Judith Sills, Ph.D, is the author of a *New York Times* bestseller, *Excess Baggage: Getting Out of Your Own Way*. Her book is a clear guide to your own personality pitfalls and a road map for steering around those of your staff and colleagues. It is equally as relevant to your self-promotion journey as it is to steering around others. We need to be able to get out of our own way. Sometimes, our own way is hard to see as it's ingrained in the fabric of our own *normal*, our habits and our standard way of seeing the world. Self-promotion will be tough if we don't examine our own socialisation and biases to see where we might be catching ourselves out.

As you read in the introduction, I grew up in a community that valued humility above all else. Wins and achievements were downplayed. We weren't supposed to stand out, but to fit in. Talent was seen as some sort of secret. I certainly felt I wasn't able to talk about my talents, but if someone 'discovered' me, that was okay. This, in turn, drove me to adopt passive ways of standing out with things like clothing, attitude and haircut, rather than standing out for doing things well.

I'm not that unusual. Many women, and some men, feel this way. Self-deprecation and self-deprecating humour are standard fare for many—especially in Australia, New Zealand and the United Kingdom.

Have you watched the Netflix documentary *Crossfit's Fittest Men and Women on Earth?* It was 2016 and Tia Toomey, who had ranked #2 the year prior, was leading the challenge and positioned at #1 on the leader board for most of the 2016 event. Tia is an amazing Australian competitor who is incredibly humble—self-deprecatingly so.

Given my interest in gender, confidence and humility, I was horrified when a fan asked for a photo and Tia replied demurely (I'm paraphrasing), 'Oh, you'll think, *who was that bitch?* when I don't win'.

She went onto rank #2 in the world again (pipped at the post) but the next year went on to rank #1. She also represented Australia in the Olympic Games. Yet, while her humility is both charming and disarming (both stereotypically appropriate options for women), I couldn't help but wonder if this was really unhelpful for younger female athletes coming up through the ranks. In this arena, Tia is a legend and role model to men and women. A mere 'thank you' would have sufficed and may have done her own self-esteem some good as well. Don't let your own baggage get in the way of your positive self-belief or let it impact the belief of others.

Add to the mix the incredible double standards for women who express their ambition, their desire to get ahead and/or who simply want a leadership career. Our society is quick off the mark to judge women on anything from appearance, to beauty regime, to whether they spend enough time with family, their tone of voice and their femininity. We don't do the same for men and these things are *not* relevant to a leadership journey.

My response? 'The double standards we walk past are the double standards we accept' to paraphrase General David Morrison again. When was the last time you criticised another woman for something that had nothing to do with her leadership capacity and more to do with her not being aligned to *femininity*? When was the last time you commented (positively or negatively) on what a female news anchor or speaker wore? The flurry of commentary around the dress choices for Megan Markel before and after the wedding are full of bias, socialisation and double standards that need to be decoded if we are going to feel more comfortable about putting ourselves out there.

Unguarded comments about women are bound to catch you out one day. Not because you'll be overheard or because others will think you are commenting wrongly (unfortunately), but these comments are an infraction against yourself. You'll be holding yourself to that same unrealistic or irrelevant standard. When we are measuring ourselves against impossible, unrealistic and double standards, we'll find ourselves less likely to give it a go.

Moving forward, we need mechanisms to regularly interrupt our thought beliefs and biases that enable us to move forward more easily.

 Activity

Rank yourself, on a scale of 1–10, on where you are on systematically managing your own beliefs and biases, and how easy it is for you to get out of your own way.

3. What do I stand for? Am I prepared to take a position?

When it comes to self-promotion, it's much easier when you have a platform on which to stand. And, no, I don't necessarily mean your *soapbox* or your *high horse*. I'm talking about a cause, a purpose, a mission or your brand. There is an old saying, *'When you stand for nothing, you fall for everything'*. When you self-promote, you want to be known for something. This could be called a platform, a position or a theme.

Research tells us that when women, in particular, self-promote around a cause, a purpose or a mission, they more easily depress the impact of the *modesty norm,* which usually makes them feel self-conscious.

Additionally, others are far more forgiving if women get it wrong or if the activity is perceived to be not as per the feminine stereotype when you are *on purpose*. This effectively circumvents negative judgments and social penalties or the *backlash effect.* A definite win/win.

In a nutshell, women are more likely to get out of their own way and flagrantly self-promote when it's for a cause, a purpose or a mission.

Your UVP

You can use your unique value proposition to self-promote. This means you need to take a position. You need to back yourself, and your ideas and claim that unique space between your experience, your expertise and those things you are most passionate about. So my question to you is this: how comfortable are you in taking a position?

Most of us cringe when remembering an uncomfortable time at a dinner party where someone dominated the conversation with their dogmatic 'position'. Let's not even go there. Simply remember the Buddhist principle of *care deeply, hold lightly* and you'll be fine. However, at the other end of the spectrum, is the person mistaken for wallpaper; they never say a thing; they fade into the background, and people wonder why they are in the room.

As a leader, or aspiring leader, being able to express your opinion and to take a position, is part and parcel of your development because it will help set the vision and bring others along on the journey.

How can I work out my position?

Here are my four go-to questions that help you work out your position on any issue:

- What do you believe about this particular issue?
- Why is this important?
- How does this add value?
- What's in it for the intended listener/audience?

In fact, you could create a presentation or LinkedIn post around those four bullet points alone, and it would go a long way to helping others remember you. Once you are comfortable articulating all four, self-promotion becomes a breeze.

Is it even worth it? Surely there are no new ideas left

Yes, it is worth it. Remember, it's not what you know or even who you know, it's who knows what you know and how that adds value. You cannot sell a secret, so you have to share your ideas with others. Sometimes a new voice can bring a fresh perspective and helps solve old problems in new ways. Diversity works, so don't even begin to think your position doesn't have any value.

Digging deep into your sense of *why* will help you do this. Why do you turn up to work every day? Why do you work in this industry? Why do you do good work? Why is this work important? Why is this perspective important? Asking yourself why is nearly always a game changer.

Letting go of the need to be right

The practice of defencelessness will make taking a position far easier for you. It means letting go of the need to be right. Add this to letting go of the need to know everything and expressing your opinion is far easier.

Jane Caro, media commentator, comedian and speaker, taught me this as I was about to head on stage in Canberra for a debate on gender salary equity. What I realised, in the hour prior to going on stage, was that my team was up against some extremely clever PhDs and journalists, and I felt like a fish out of water. The best bit? Her advice was fabulous. Once I let go of the need to be right and focused instead on what I bring to the table (humour, insight, perspective), my team won the day.

Quick and easy wins

Here are some quick and easy tactics to try once you've worked out what you stand for:

- Take a stand and express your opinion in meetings where you normally let others do all the talking.
- Provide smart and persuasive commentary at an event or ask a smart question from the back of the room.
- Craft a compelling argument in an online forum.
- Comment 'on brand' on other people's LinkedIn posts.
- Publish or post 'on brand' on LinkedIn.
- Create an opportunity for decision makers to see what you represent and that you have value to add. Don't let your boss get all the opportunities and subsequent glory.

When the rubber hits the road

Once you've worked out what you stand for and have a road map for helping yourself to stand out for all the right reasons, place an appointment (with yourself) in your calendar to ensure it starts today. Practice makes perfect and you have to start somewhere.

 Activity

Rank yourself on a scale of 1–10 based on where you are on that journey.

1 = I've done nothing.

5 = I know what I stand for; I've done the work; I've got ideas that I never share and as a result I'm a secret weapon.

10 = I've done the work; everyone knows about me and what I have to offer. In fact, I'm highly sought after to contribute on those platforms. Plus, I'm invited to commentate on other things because people respect my insights so highly.

4. How well do you proactively nurture confidence, manage stress and prioritise wellbeing?

There is a Buddhist saying that might be wise to remember, 'You should sit in meditation for twenty minutes every day, unless you're too busy; and then you should sit for an hour.'

It's hard to self-promote or take a public position when you don't feel good about yourself. In fact, it's hard to do anything particularly well when you're worn out. Stress is a huge underminer of wellbeing, self-worth and self-confidence. If you're anything like me, if you're stressed or over- stretched, you'll most likely want to hide away rather than of a head to a networking function or write your next *think* piece for LinkedIn or your blog.

In mid-2018, I was invited to speak to a group of female CEOs and managing directors. I posed this same question to them (How well do you proactively nurture confidence, manage stress and prioritise wellbeing?) and was delighted to hear they all prioritised practices. They all scored a 9 or a 10 for prioritising their mental and physical wellbeing. In fact, they all said they simply couldn't lead well if they didn't.

Ideas to help you

How well do you prioritise your mental fitness with tools like meditation, mindfulness, gardening or other? (Yes, gardening has been shown to have a dramatic therapeutic benefit for mental health and wellbeing.)

Do you have a regular gratitude practice? Practising gratitude, according to science, is a brain changer as it changes the way your brain is wired. It's a game changer for me and goes something like this: each morning, identify five things for which you feel grateful. Don't just write them down, allow the sensation of gratitude to wash through your body and brain. Then each evening, note five things you did well. I find this particularly relevant if I've had a bad day, feel exhausted or had someone make a complaint. Notice how this flicks a switch of change in your self-worth and well-being.

Do you *harvest* oxytocin? Oxytocin is a stress buster. Ideas include daily hugs, cuddles, spending time appreciating your children/ significant other (if relevant), playing with pets. In fact, the entire 'rom com' movie genre could make a comeback if people understood that it helped them feel good about themselves. Allegedly, baby cat and baby goat videos also work. (I go gaga for a baby sloth video.) Perhaps this practice is for you.

How well do you prioritise physical movement? Movement is medicine. It doesn't have to be a 10K+ run. In fact, researchers have found that over exercisers can have higher inflammation markers in their body, which leads to increased stress. Regularly standing up from your desk, exercise in a variety of intensities, team sports, walking, cycling, swimming, tai chi, Yoga. Whatever it is, just move.

Do you know your 'why'? Aligning yourself to a deeper sense of why or purpose will not only help you get out of your way, but also help you manage stress more easily. If you're self-promoting for a cause, vision or purpose that isn't in alignment with you, you'll struggle and feel even more stressed. I don't mean you need to quit your day job. Carolyn Tate, author of *The Purpose Project* (2017) says, 'For many of us, doing work that fulfils our purpose seems like an impossibility. We've bought into the erroneous belief that we must flee our job (and life) to go in search of our why in some other job or company or as an entrepreneur'. Finding a sense of why inside your role and organisation might be the very thing that helps you reduce stress or get out of your comfort zone more easily.

Do you have easy go-to strategies for breaking the cycle of worry or anxiety? And I don't mean alcohol as that's a short-term fix. Clients have shared these tactics with me: walking on the beach with their feet in the sand or water, having a shower, smelling herbs or aromatherapy, cooking, gardening or helping someone else. My standard strategy is Yoga Nidra. It stops my negative thoughts in their tracks. There is a range of tactics you might use. Find one that works for you. Staying in a loop of anxiety will help no-one and will keep you from self-promoting.

If you're leaning out of self-promoting, doing this work might be the very thing you need to do more of.

 Activity

Rank yourself on a scale of 1–10 based on how proactively you manage the above.

1 = I don't have any regular or scheduled practices. I know I should but I never understood how important it was.

5 = I have practices that I do mostly but when I get stressed I forget them all.

10 = Stress and wellbeing management is my superpower. I not only have a 30-minute daily practice but I have regular interventions I can try during the day that act as a circuit-breaker when things get out of hand.

5. How well do you handle feedback, criticism and commentary?

There's no getting past it. When you put yourself, your ideas, thoughts and IP out there, you run the risk of criticism. However, don't forget that you also run the risk of getting great feedback, positive acclaim and you can help others more effectively if they know how to find you. As one of my Rockstar clients says, 'if you don't have any haters, you haven't self-promoted hard enough'.

Feedback, criticism (constructive or other), commentary and resistance to your ideas are a given. And if it's not, you're not self-promoting hard enough. We live in a world where we've forgotten how to have discourse to persuade and influence. Instead, everything seems black or white, good or bad, right or wrong. Learning and accepting feedback, commentary and resistance is all part and parcel of growth and development.

Janelle Barlow wrote a book called *The Complaint is a Gift* (2008). It comes from the customer service world and examines how the information gleaned from complaints is so very helpful in improving your service offerings and fixing problems. It also has the potential to create brand advocates. It was radical thinking in its day and based on the evolution of corporate, government and business, it's still relevant today. But most of us hate complaints. We dislike criticism, feedback and those who reject our ideas. If I had a dollar for the number of times I've heard people talk about how much they dislike the dreaded performance appraisal, I'd be super rich.

However, in the self-promotion game, you can expect others to:

- Reject or challenge some of your ideas.
- Have a perspective that's different to your own.
- Criticise your ideas in a way that's hurtful.
- Try to take you down because you are standing out.
- Think you're 'big noting' yourself however subtle your self-promotion tactics are.

You need to be ready. I'm a big believer in taking charge of this to mitigate the damage. Place controls around when you look at online forums (where your ideas might be published). No late night looking at comments on LinkedIn—you may not be sleeping now but you'll likely sleep less after accidentally finding a comment you didn't agree with.

Do the work in advance to prepare your responses to the sorts of criticisms you might receive. It's amazing how much more confident you feel when you've pre-prepared. Other tactics include developing your resilience muscle with a quick round of *The Rejection Game* (the more times you hear 'no' the closer you are to a 'yes'). Some *Failure Practice* wouldn't go astray either. Find something to do that you're likely to fail at and go do it!

Finally, letting go of the need to be perfect, to be liked by everyone, to know everything, and to be right, will help you become more resilient around feedback.

 Activity

Rank yourself on a scale of 1–10 based on where you are on that journey.

1 = I actively avoid feedback. I hate giving it and hate receiving it. I cry at performance appraisal time, and I hate giving feedback in case the recipient doesn't like me.

5 = I'm okay with feedback but I get nervous about commenting on LinkedIn or at forums and events in case someone doesn't like my opinion, or I make a mistake in a public way.

10 = I'm a total Rockstar with feedback. I have responses in my back pocket if I get trolled on social media; I welcome real debate or commentary around my ideas because that's where new ideas come from; I seek opportunities to talk to those with different opinions as this helps me understand how to create persuasive counter arguments or rethink my own ideas.

6. Career strategy

Do you put your career success down to plain luck or a plan? If it's a plan, might you be able to call it a career strategy?

According to the 2018 *Women CEOs Speak* study (Korn Ferry, 2018):

- 65% of female CEOs surveyed said they only realised they could become a CEO after someone told them so.
- Only 12% said they had aspired to a CEO role for a long time.

Startling!

In a nutshell, many executive women, including those already leading, don't aspire to become the boss. Rather:

- they don't aim for the top job.
- they don't believe it's a viable option for them.
- they don't plan for the possibility of getting there.

But if you don't know where you are going, how will you know when you get there?

Figure 3: Career strategy is the missing 33% for many women

I've got a theory. I call it the missing 33%. We don't teach young women and girls about the importance of having a career strategy. We teach women about work and we teach women about the importance of having an identity outside of work. But the career strategy is the missing piece of the puzzle. Do we formally teach young boys something different? Not necessarily. But they have far more visible male role models making plans to lead, and succeeding, creating part of the education process for boys. Plus, I suspect boys are far less self-conscious about not hitting targets or looking like a fool if they don't get there.

Back to you. Do you have a bold and exciting plan for your career or future? Once again, it's far easier to self-promote if you know why you are doing it, where you are going and how you need to get there.

Activity

Rank yourself on a scale of 1–10 based on where you are on that journey.

1 = I have nothing. I lurch from one job to the other with no real plan in mind.

5 = I sort of have a plan but I hate sharing it because if it doesn't work out, I don't want to look like a failure. It's more of a wish list rather than a plan.

10 = I have a future focused, career strategy in place. I have shared it with key people in my life to support me getting there. I've addressed gaps, risks, threats and opportunities. I know what I'm doing, where I'm going and how I'm going to get there.

 Case study

Olivia had a 'head of' role. She was talented, innovative and ready for the next level. While getting feedback about her resume, a male peer noted she didn't have any direct P&L experience and suggested if she wanted a C-suite role, it would be perceived as a gap.

This feedback resonated. She is not alone. Many women have come up through disciplines that don't have direct P&L remit. She knew enough not to feel bad or to stop aiming for the C-suite, so instead she did something about it. She continued putting herself forward for assignments, projects and opportunities with more P&L responsibility: volunteering, asking, offering and talking about this requirement—not just during her annual performance review but at other times also.

I'm delighted to announce after two years, Olivia landed a juicy role with direct P&L responsibility. All of a sudden, the C-suite role she was aiming for was far closer than she originally imagined.

7.   Visibility strategy

Are you seen and heard in the right places? Visibility is the one key element that gets in the way for many of my senior level clients. You have to be seen, not just in the right places, but by the right people, with the right key message, at the right time, in the right company and all in alignment with your future career goals.

Your visibility strategy can be made up of the following types of visible activities:

Internal visibility with those inside the organisation (formal meetings, one-on-one meetings, being seen around the office by the right people).

- Staff
- Peers
- Internal stakeholders
- Decision makers
- Your internal champions and sponsors.

External visibility with those outside the organisation (conferences, meetings, events).

- Stakeholders
- Customers/clients
- Industry peers
- Industry decision makers
- Your external champions and sponsors.

Online visibility which can cut across both internal and external and has the ability to go far wider. LinkedIn or other professional platforms enable you to create a presence and brand for yourself online so you not only have a professional digital footprint, but you can be found for all the right search terms.

Most importantly, you want to link your visibility activities to your career strategy. You aren't just connecting with people for the sake of collecting connections. Instead, you are keeping your eye on your long-term career goals and ensuring you fit your own mask first (so to speak). For those with a tendency to be the loyal, hardworking Workhorse, this can feel uncomfortable. However, if you reframe this into something that's helpful for you in your current role, you'll be in a position to help more people or solve more problems in a different role. After all, you can't be seen, heard and valued if no-one knows about you. If you are invisible, you can't potentially apply your unique blend of enthusiasm, experience and expertise in new or different situations.

Strategic networking counts

Lets talk about networking, specifically strategic networking in alignment with your future aspirations and career goals. In April 2018, *HBR* published an article that stated CEOs with diverse networks create higher firm value, 'Diversely networked CEOs generated an approximately sixteenfold firm market value increase relative to their compensation'.

Yes, that's right. Diverse networks—breadth, not necessarily depth. Put that together with what is already well known, 'firms with better-connected CEOs can obtain cheaper financing, and firms with well-connected board directors see better performance,' and you begin to see that networking is not just great for you and your career, it's great for the divisions you lead and the organisations for which you work.

Picture this ....

At one end of the networking spectrum there is *Nigella No-Friends.* She's busy. Give Nigella something to do, and she does it well. Nigella is incredibly conscientious, diligent and hardworking. She is reliable and available, and doesn't have time or energy to invest in strategic networking. 'Who has time for networking?' she cries. She is too busy being head down, backside up, cleaning up after everyone else. She truly believes that if she wasn't there to do the job she is doing, the project/program/organisation would fail. She knows it's working short term for the organisation, but deep down she knows it's not working long term for herself. Yet, she doesn't know another way.

At the other end of the spectrum is *Garry* (name changed to protect the innocent). Garry is the CFO of an ASX listed organisation, and I affectionately name him *Gantt Chart Garry* because he takes the notion of strategic networking to a whole new level by running a Gantt Chart on his professional networking activity. Not only does he schedule his activity over several years but he ranks his network on their net worth and how helpful they have been. He tracks where and when he last saw them, what was discussed and how helpful they may be in the future. Then he schedules ... and, boy, does he schedule. Breakfast, lunch and after-work drinks, five days per week. Oh my. Yes, he exists. And yes, he is incredibly successful in his career. And if the research on the value of strategic networking is true, then he is also incredibly valuable in the C-suite of the organisations for which he works. This approach helps him deliver better results.

Now I'm not saying, for a minute, that everyone needs to set up a CRM or Gantt Chart for their networking strategy. There's probably not much room in that approach for emotional intelligence, intuition and ad hoc encounters. But somewhere in between *Nigella* and *Garry*, there is a strategy or plan that's right for you—a *sweet spot* that enables you to balance a heavy workload, family obligations, career and leadership aspirations along with your discomfort with networking, the modesty effect and other socialised stereotyped norms.

Your sweet spot might just prioritise things that deliver far more return on investment, help you maintain your confidence and mojo plus enable to you to be seen, heard and valued by people with clout or decision makers

Remember, if you are uncomfortable with something, if you link it to your deeper 'why', you'll be more likely to do it. And if it's in alignment with your goals, there's even more reason why.

 Activity

Rank yourself on a scale of 1–10 based on where you are on that journey.

1 = Just like Nigella No-Friends, you don't have time or energy for getting out to see and be seen. You weren't even aware people did that.

5 = You get out and about but in an ad hoc way. You know both networking and visibility are important but haven't worked out how to use them yet.

10 = You could show Gantt Chart Garry a thing or two. Not only do you have a visibility strategy and networking plan in place, you also apply the feminine leadership superpowers of active listening, clear communication and emotional intelligence to ensure you are seen, heard, valued and remembered.

8. How good are you at speaking to your results?

As you read earlier, results don't necessarily speak for themselves. You need to learn to speak to them, about them, to share key learnings or the benefits of the outcome. Do this regularly. It should come as no secret to your boss or your boss's boss, that you've delivered on a project and it was awesome, because you've regularly updated them about progress, key wins and learnings.

Many people hesitate to do this; they still believe they shouldn't need to speak up. Speaking about outcomes, results, impact, projects, value or the difference you make isn't bragging. It's bringing people along for the journey. To make this easier for you, reframe it into how you help others, the enterprise, your division and the industry. For example, if I worked in the fitness industry and I helped people manage their weight, by sharing some of the results, I could show just how much I could help others. In fact, the fitness or weight loss industries are great examples of where speaking to results is standard fare. We're addicted to before and after shots, then hearing about the hard work, the secret tactics and any easy wins.

So why is it okay in the fitness industry and not in others? Even thinking about talking about your wins and achievements can be an absolute minefield. However, expecting your results to speak for themselves is very passive. Learning to share your results is proactively taking charge; it's co-creating your own destiny, which may be the very destiny others had in mind for you. Plus, it builds your credibility in the eyes of the listener and you get to help more people.

In a world where others seem to name- (or achievement) drop easily, it can feel a little overwhelming but there are tactics you can use:

- Use a humble brag elevator pitch formula that finishes with a recent or relevant example of where you did something similar. Keep it brief, conversational, storytelling in style and finish with a result.
- Next time you're invited to speak at a conference or meeting, write your own bio for the person who introduces you. Include a couple of your key wins and write it in the 3rd person perspective. This gives you bonus points because it sounds like someone else is saying this about you.
- In a job interview, nearly all of your responses should include specific details about projects or initiatives with results

attached. This makes the interviewer feel more certain you've done something similar before.

- In a meeting, when asked to respond to a particular initiative, reframe so you do a quick recap with an 'achievement bomb' and include a result on a previous initiative, before responding with the relevant information. *'You may remember that last week 'x, y, z' happened and I/we were able to deliver this result. The next step is what I want to talk about today.'*

Do speak to the value of the results, the impact, the outcome, the measure, the difference made, the effect, the consequence and the upshot. If you can, put a number on it; quantify as best you can, and if you can't quantify, qualify.

I read many resumes (most from women but some from men). There is a significant difference in the way men and women tackle resume writing. Many women don't seem to collect quantifiable evidence, yet this is the language recruiting companies find most impressive, especially if working in business or corporate. Interestingly, most resumes I read from men bullet-point lists with quantifiable evidence but very little narrative or context. You need both, but demonstrable measurable outcomes are a must.

If you're not speaking to your results, keeping people abreast of project progress and critical milestones, you leave yourself open to others being credited with your results or taking credit for your work. I continually hear stories from women who are angry or frustrated that others are receiving accolades and acknowledgement (because the boss assumed or simply didn't know) or that someone blatantly took the credit for outcomes they had nothing, or very little, to do with. As bad as these situations are, if we hadn't simply been minding our own business, trying to prove how good we are by doing great work, instead of *tooting our own horn* strategically and systematically, this couldn't have happened.

 Activity

Rank yourself on a scale of 1–10 based on where you are on that journey.
1 = I hate speaking to my results and shouldn't have to do it either. I don't have any results to speak about anyway.
5 = I do it in interviews but never in any other context.
8 = I do it sometimes but not as often as I should because I know I sound like I'm bragging.
10 = I regularly and skilfully talk about achievements, outcomes and results. It never sounds like bragging because I always frame it up to be helpful to others and believe they will benefit from the insights or learnings. I can't believe how much this has helped my career, but it sure has.

Now you've come to the end of this section, tally up how you went. Total score is 80. How did you track? Above 50 is pretty good, in my opinion, because we know that women tend to underestimate their capabilities. You probably rate a little higher than you've given yourself credit for. However, take another look and then start journalling or reflecting on the following:

- Which was your highest score?
- How might that help you stand out in a crowded market place?
- Which was your lowest score?
- How might that be hindering your career?
- Work down the list again and identify one thing you can do differently from each of your four lowest scores.
- Put a plan in place to do them, then track your progress.

Don't forget the value of low hanging fruit. You don't have to target the most challenging aspects first. After all, it's progress you are looking for, not perfection.

CHAPTER 5

BRANDING, VISIBILITY AND NETWORKING HELP YOUR SELF-PROMOTION EFFORTS

Take charge of the narrative, before it takes charge of you.

We've all got a brand—whether we want one, whether we know it and whether we like it.

And you get to choose the degree …

Rolls Royce vs Dodgy Brothers
The Queen's Corgi vs a bitsa
Prada vs Kmart
Krug vs Great Western

Or anywhere in between.

Don't be a victim or passive recipient of your brand. Instead, be a co-creator of your own reality.

Take charge of the narrative before it takes charge of you

Now that you've done the mini audit, it's time to start pulling a plan together. My wish for you is to discover what gets in the way of your self-promotion efforts and to create your own self-promotion strategy.

My favourite piece of advice for clients is *take charge of the narrative before it takes charge of you.* This comes from my experience running executive branding workshops, but is equally valid in a self-promotion setting.

Don't let other people's opinions dictate your success. Self-promotion, in and of itself, is a proactive tactic. It gets you on the front foot. No more being a passive recipient of whatever unfolds in your career, what others think of you, or whether you are a success. Instead, become an active co-creator of your own existence and reality.

Sounds a bit *woo woo* doesn't it? Certainly clichéd. But what happens if this is true? Instead of waiting for others to tell you if you're any good, learn to objectively measure and discuss your own results. Instead of waiting for others to give you opportunities, create them. It's not wrong. It's not even cheeky. It's what most highly successful and entrepreneurial people do. You can't imagine that Naomi Simson (Red Balloon Days), Janine Allis (Boost Juice) or Melanie Perkins (Canva) waited in the wings for other people to give them permission to be successful. No. They went about creating their own success.

 Case study

Sophie was a young, talented woman and felt stifled in her role. She had an extremely valuable skillset (she was great at sales) and no matter how hard she tried to change, shift or do something slightly different, the organisation simply kept her there *because* she was so good at sales.

She decided to try and further her career outside of the organisation, not in a disloyal way but via her industry association. She still held down her day job, but on the side, she proactively took part in activities the association had to offer. In fact, she was so proactive and successful that she ended up with Chairing and Award responsibilities and was on several high profile committees. This led to media exposure, industry-wide exposure, board and governance training, P&L exposure, and other leadership opportunities that enhanced her career and made it all the more rewarding. Plus, her work colleagues started seeing her in an entirely different way. She definitely took charge of the narrative before it took charge of her.

Now it's your turn

- How can you take charge of your career narrative before it takes charge of you?
- How can you proactively get on the front foot and tackle the ups, downs and sideways moves in your career journey and turn them into something you love or are really proud of?

The model below brings the research, methodology and philosophy together in a way that enables you to self-promote more effectively.

- No more missing out on perfect opportunities because you were a legend in your own lunch box yet no-one else's.
- No more missing out on plum assignments because you were too busy cleaning up after everyone else.
- No more being dismissed as lightweight because you look good, young, pretty or simply different, and people make assumptions about you.
- No more feeling like a pretender or a fraud.

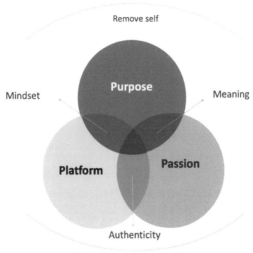

Figure 4: The eight pillars of self-promotion

Why? Because each item on the model will help you navigate your way through your own socialisation and biases, to navigate the modesty norm, societal expectations around the feminine, standing out, bragging and feeling like an imposter. This next session is your road map.

Removing self

My second favourite piece of advice is to *take the* self *out of* self-*promotion*. When we remove ourselves from the equation and make it about being in service to others, for the benefit of others, we are far more likely to self-promote. No bragging here, but be helpful instead.

Ask yourself:

- How can I remove myself from the equation yet still get the credit?

- How can I make this less about me and more about being in service to others?
- Does my work help others in some way?
- Does my work help my organisation in some way?

Once we become less self-conscious, and more focused on others, self-promotion becomes a cinch.

PURPOSE is important when it comes to self-promotion. As you learned in Chapter 1, and again earlier in Chapter 2, it is much easier to self-promote, when it's aligned with your sense of purpose. For some, the reason they work is to provide for their family unit. If that's you, your self-promotion efforts will help you win pay rises more easily, so it's a win/win. When they reframe self-promotion activities around their 'why' like ensuring their kids live in a safe neighbourhood, get a good education or have more opportunities, they're far more likely to self-promote with ease. It's not for themselves; it's for their kids. Not selfish at all.

For others, purpose might be aligned with the type of work they do. For example, if you were a yoga teacher helping people to live healthy, happy and long lives, then why would you not self-promote? You can help more people when you self-promote because students can find you.

In fact, I spent three years administering a Facebook group of over 1000 yoga teachers. Despite the stereotype of yoga teachers not being attached to material wealth, I've never come across an industry who self-promoted more. Or perhaps I noticed it more because I had beliefs that aligned with the stereotype. Why did they self-promote? 1. Because, frequently, yoga teachers are paid on a commission basis; therefore, being paid is a good motivator. 2. They firmly believed in the value and benefit of their offering. They helped people be happier and healthier physically, mentally and emotionally every day, and they knew it.

By self-promoting for a purpose, or a 'why', you are, once again, removing yourself from the equation and that makes it easier. When your self-promotion activities are more aligned with your sense of purpose, a deeper 'why', it will feel like a piece of cake.

 Activity

Take a moment and reflect on the following:

What's important to me about work? How will self-promoting help achieve that goal? How will not self-promoting impact that goal? Who else benefits from the work I do? How will self-promoting help them? If I don't self-promote who might this harm?

PASSION is a powerful driver and a big lever to help you get out of your own way and self-promote. Passion not only depresses the *Modesty Norm* but it also buys you a second chance. People are more forgiving of someone who breaches prescribed socialised or stereotyped norms, when they are passionate about the cause. There is the added benefit in that those who are passionate about something are more likely to do it anyway and not worry about what others think. Plus, when we speak with natural enthusiasm and excitement, we are frequently far more persuasive. Candidates in job interviews, who are naturally enthusiastic in their responses, do better than those who aren't. Those who display natural enthusiasm and passion when pitching for seed funding are often more successful than those who do not.

While you might be sitting there thinking *I'm not passionate about work; it just pays the bills and is a hard slog most of the time*, there may be some aspect of your work that you can get passionate about: a special project, a committee or an opportunity that's afforded you because someone else learned about how talented you are in a particular area. Perhaps you are bored by the day-to-day account management, but you are beginning to love helping your staff deliver better results. Perhaps managing your technology team used to be what got you out of bed in the morning, but now it's all a bit humdrum. However, there is a side project running at head office that you've been wanting to get involved in—that really gets you excited again.

Look beyond the humdrum or the slog of your everyday role to find the juice that will enable you to showcase yourself, talk about the problems you solve, the difference you make and the value you add with natural flair and enthusiasm.

 Activity

Take a moment and reflect on the following:

What area of my work am I passionate about? Where do I naturally display enthusiasm and excitement, and how can I create opportunities to talk about the issues at work that really light me up?
If I can't find that in my current role, where else (inside or outside my organisation) can I find those things that light my professional fire again? What will get me back to talking enthusiastically about outcomes, results and value that I've delivered?
Is there an issue (I feel passionate about) that I could write about and share on LinkedIn or speak about at conferences?

Having a **PLATFORM** makes it far, far easier to self-promote. A platform could be a unique position, a cause or a base on which to stand or leverage, or a perspective that represents your values. It is an excellent depressant of the *Modesty Norm*. You are less likely to be criticised, when it's on behalf of a cause or if it delivers social benefit to a charity.

 Case study

Vicky is a client. She is normally a *best kept secret* but, one day, when she heard her boss talking about a secondment opportunity for a national staff training roadshow, she threw her hat in the ring. Even though the thought of being on stage scared her, she knew she loved educating others and the new initiatives she was training on (in her current role) provided her a great platform. Of course, she asked for support and training herself in order to do a great job. After all, it was in the organisation's best interests to see the initiative succeed.

The result? At the end of her secondment, Vicky had developed a new skillset. She discovered that while she would never really love the spotlight, when she reframed it in terms of educating and helping others, she was quite good at it. Due to the nature of the project, she also had to report on outcomes of the program to the C-suite, which in turn got her noticed in all the right places.

Benefits to her personally?
She was now known by far more people at all levels, throughout the national enterprise.
She had a brand and reputation of being far more confident than she felt; her stage presence stood her in good stead.
This led to a choice of plum assignments in the future, plus a significant pay rise as a result of the entire project.
And while she wasn't exactly self-promoting on the tour, the platform of the roadshow provided her a great reason to showcase herself in a different way. It gained her high level visibility and that's a bonus (Orbach, 2006).

Activity

Take a moment and reflect on the following:

What sort of platform could I leverage inside or outside of my organisation? It could even be online.

Is there a cause that helps others that I could get behind? Maybe it's a fundraising initiative at work, or the staff awards committee or a cross departmental project?

Is there an industry committee such as an awards, standards review or conference organising committee I can get involved with that will enable me to showcase myself and my expertise in a different way in front of a bigger and broader audience?

Once you've found your platform, share the impact of your contribution to ensure you're not pigeonholed as a Workhorse but as someone who delivers substantive value. Don't keep it a secret. Talk about your work.

The sweet spot

This is where Purpose, Passion and Platform collide. When your sense of 'why' is engaged, you get to display natural enthusiasm for the work and where the cause or platform is bigger than you. Find this spot so you can speak about your results, and share stories, insights and impact. It will become a natural part of your conversation and role.

Let's keep going ...

Finding **MEANING** helps self-promotion become more palatable. We are in a world where sales and marketing has moved towards providing information. This is a shift you can also make in your self-promotion activities. We live in an information economy, where those able to make *meaning* out of new ideas, thought leadership and information are highly sought after. Replace 'Look at *moi*' with the far more helpful 'I'm helping others make sense of what's going on in the world' or 'I'm sharing my results, findings and insights to help others make sense of the world'.

But once again, you need to share your *meaning* making, asking for feedback and commentary on your perspective and ideas. We are talking about self-promotion activities, so it's not enough to have ideas written down in a private journal. You need to be prepared to share, discuss, debate and deliberate on your ideas with others.

Ideas:

- Coordinating a 'lunch and learn' at work to help others understand what's going on in your division.
- Publishing articles, blogs or white papers on your intranet, LinkedIn or through your peak body.
- Put your hand up to do a 5-minute presentation on a project you are passionate about to ensure others in the department can get up to speed faster.
- Invite yourself to be on panel discussions or speak at conferences.
- Throw your hat in the ring to be interviewed on podcasts or panels. Once again, not so you can say *look at how good I am* but instead, *I'm helping others make sense of this complicated issue.*

Self-promotion feels like a walk in the park for those who enjoy making and sharing meaning.

We've touched on **MINDSET** in the previous chapter. When it comes to self-promotion, maintaining a positive Growth or Possibility Mindset is critical to the self-promotion task and all other aspects of your leadership or career journey. Unfortunately, the small voice that says 'I can't do that' gets louder and insistent when we're tired, feeling rejected or outside our comfort zone. For many, spruiking for 'brand you' *will* be outside your comfort zone; however, if you approach self-promotion with a Growth and Possibility Mindset, it becomes a breeze.

Showing **AUTHENTICITY** is exactly as it sounds; it's using *your* voice with real examples, real language, minimal jargon or formal language, and real attitude. You're simply talking about the outcomes of your work, far more strategically and with more deliberate intent. There's nothing worse than feeling inauthentic while selling 'brand you'.

A classic example would be at a job interview. Likely you are:

- Dressed to the nines in your best outfit; you feel slightly uncomfortable; your shoes are too high; your makeup is heavier than usual.
- Pretending to laugh at all the jokes even though it feels like you're being grilled on the stand.
- Minding your Ps and Qs.
- Giving rehearsed answers, regurgitating annual report-type language or balancing trying to impress with jargon while making it all seem oh so natural.

Researchers agree that you win the interviews where you feel as though you are having a conversation with a peer. In 2018, researchers looked at the link between authenticity and power and found that authenticity drives the authenticity-to-power effect, helps us make better decisions and increases the likelihood of being an effective negotiator and leader. Wow. (Gan, Heller, & Chen, 2018).

Does being authentic mean letting it all hang out? Not at all. Professional standards and courtesy are a given. But within that there is wriggle room to bring your more authentic self to the table. In fact, when it comes to self-promotion, you'll be more effective when it's a congruent version of you. Self-promotion becomes a doddle when you feel (in)credible and you'll have far more impact if you're being authentic.

CHAPTER 6

VISIBILITY AND NETWORKING

**'Your brand is what others say about you when
you are not in the room'.—Jeff Bezos**

When I started my consultancy I had a branding problem. I'd been in the business of making other people look good but no-one knew who I was. Including myself. I was almost invisible. I was The Enabler. And was far more comfortable working in the background than in the limelight.

So with determination, trial and error, and a big sense of purpose, I built a brand on LinkedIn.
I inspired women to step up, speak out and STAND OUT.

In order to do that, I had to get way out of my comfort zone and stand out all on my own.

That was something I found terrifying but grew more comfortable with over time.

Today, I have 19K+ connections on LinkedIn and blog following. I speak regularly to audiences around Australia and inspire them to refine their executive brand and to take charge of their career narrative before it takes charge of them.

Why not ditch that worry and ensure your brand positions you to get invitations into the room in the first place?

Stop being busy, start being strategic

As you've already learned, visibility is really important. Now, let's learn more about creating a visibility strategy.

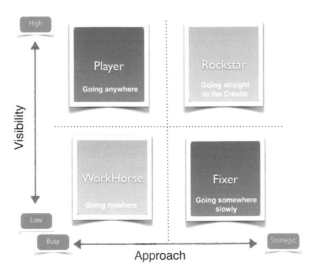

Figure 5: Build out your visibility strategy

Your approach: Busy vs Strategic (bottom axis)

> *'Self-promotion doesn't have to be an all or nothing activity. Be selective on the channels you choose and how you do it. That can make it easier to manage.'*
>
> —Susan Steele

I'm a big believer in taking a deliberate and strategic approach to your career. After all, if you don't know where you are going, how will you know when you get there? For many of us, we've spent most of our life picking up the pieces, following the rules, or trying things that others have told us to, so we're not sure what really works. We're already super busy with the bulk of home responsibilities in addition to managing a career with substance. Alternatively, we're feeling a little under-confident in new arenas, which leads to us compensating with *brand busy*. We don't know what really works, so we try everything. We get overwhelmed because we can't decipher what to stop doing ... so we stop everything. It's now time to become far more strategic in your approach.

Your visibility: Low to high visibility (vertical axis)

You cannot sell a secret. You need to become visible and stand out from the crowd for all the right reasons. Ask yourself: How visible am I to senior level decision makers, influencers, people who have clout? How visible am I internally, externally and online?

One challenge for those who work in multi-national organisations with an offshore focus is they don't have much visibility here in Australia, unless they work at it. When it comes to landing a new role back in Australia, it's almost as though they are starting from scratch unless they've been active at mitigating that in some way or another. And although working from home may be highly desirable, being seen around the office can provide a significant advantage. You cannot sell a secret, so having high visibility is important.

Some of the labels below are familiar; you came across them in a previous model. But that's okay because it all dovetails together.

Strategic visibility

The Workhorse. Give a busy woman something to do and she'll get it done. If you're a Workhorse, you've probably had values of hard work and determination drummed into you throughout your life. There is nothing wrong with hard work and determination. In fact, they are admiral traits, but if that's all you're known for you'll quickly become stuck, frustrated and disillusioned. You run the risk of being replaced by software. Be sure to ditch the Workhorse brand sooner rather than later or you'll be stuck *going nowhere*.

As Caterina Fake says 'Working on the right thing is probably more important than working hard'. But the Workhorse either doesn't know that, or deep down doesn't agree.

The Player. Some people are simply in the right place at the right time, all the time. They are well networked, know everyone and are at the opening of an envelope. However, they run the risk of people wondering if they're a lightweight because no-one really knows why they are in the room. If this is you, ask yourself three things:

- What do I stand for?
- Why is that important?
- How does it add value?

Be able to articulate your answers clearly to shift towards the Rockstar; otherwise, you'll end up not really in charge of you own destiny but at the whim of forces around you.

The Fixer is my favourite brand. They are definitely strategic; they know where they are going and make deliberate approaches and attempts to get there. As a reformed Fixer, it takes one to know one. Many of my clients hail from this category with a unique blend of experience, expertise and emotional intelligence that enables them to solve complex nuanced problems involving people, operations and strategy. However, someone else will get the glory because the Fixer is hidden; they miss being in the room at the right time.

Key lessons for the Fixer? Become more visible and learn how to self-promote. You already understand strategy, so use it to ensure you are seen, heard and valued:

- by the right people
- at the right time
- in the right place
- with the right key messages
- in the right currency or palette.

The right currency or palette is important because success and leadership is so closely correlated with those who have height, a deeper voice, and are named Peter, that making sure you're speaking their language is necessary. After all, I wouldn't begin a presentation to a mining organisation boardroom dominated by men with an Oprah Winfrey quote—no matter how well known she is.

Obviously the Fixer feels frustrated, gets sidelined for projects she thought she was a shoo-in for, and is frequently flabbergasted as she watches a (possibly) younger Player, who she didn't even know was in the running, walk away with the glory and reward. And while the Fixer is going somewhere, it's a slow row to hoe, and they are likely to pick up their bat and ball and leave before too long.

The Rockstar self-promotor status is where you are aiming (with national or international recognition). You are highly sought after, your expertise and thought leadership is well known in industry and beyond, and you execute branded self-promotion strategies with seemingly effortless ease. The following are key for the Rockstar:

- Everyone knows what you stand for, why that's important and how it adds value—not just to the organisation but industry more broadly.
- You know how to pick your battles; people know exactly what you represent.
- You are also known for playing a long and strategic game. After all the Rolling Stones are still going strong.

- You've got access to the hallowed hall of decision makers (you're a sought after decision maker yourself).
- You know what the right time, place, audience, key message and currency is because the Rockstar is integral to setting the agenda in the first place.

How are you seen by the right people, in the right place, at the right time, and with the right key messages in the right currency? You use the model below to put a strategic plan together until this becomes your new normal.

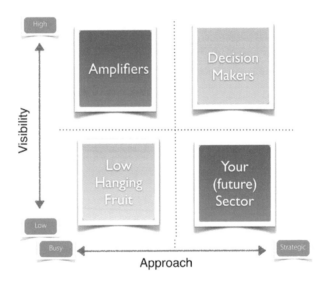

Figure 6: Power up your networking

The problem with being a collaborative problem solver (for women and their careers)

As a Fixer or a Workhorse, you run the risk of being out of line of sight from decision makers. This is a far bigger problem for women than men because we've been socialised to believe that in order to get ahead we need to do great work and that the work itself will speak to our success.

Unfortunately, this isn't true for most and the end result is that women end up wearing a cloak of invisibility. The business doesn't want to disturb them while they go about solving enormous business problems (governance, compliance, transformational change or reputational risk); therefore, someone more ambitious and more *visible* will overtake and/or bypass them. The added layer of complexity is that this hard work, paying more attention to detail and relying on being highly organised, can leave them so tired and worn out, that they don't make time for networking. It's, therefore, important that you begin strategically building a plan that includes a networking strategy with the right audience, in the right places, at the right time and … oh yes, BYO right key messages—even while you solve those big problems within the business.

It's a well-known fact that I dislike networking—I'd rather go to the dentist. Sure, that's an exaggeration but there is quite a bit of truth in it, and I'm an extrovert. Imagine being an introvert and feeling as though you need to attend networking functions all the time. Most of us have far better things to do with our time; however, when you plan right and create networking opportunities that work for you, then you'll do great, whether an introvert or an extravert.

I encourage you to use is the *Power up your networking* model above. It will help you work out where you need to spend time in a range of areas. It's got the same labels as the previous *Build out your visibility strategy* model, so you're beginning to get the picture.

Low hanging fruit are those easy-to-make connections. For example:

- when you upload your connections into LinkedIn.

- when LinkedIn suggests people to you.
- when you bump into someone at a random networking function.
- the people on your table, or who you happen to meet.

It's great to have some Low Hanging Fruit in the mix. It's fun, encourages diversity and keeps life interesting. I wouldn't recommend relying on it as a strategy to get ahead; unless you choose said networking functions wisely, you won't get very far, and you need to add more visibility and more strategy for that.

Amplifiers are highly visible and well networked. They are your brand advocates or are simply happy to help. Frequently, the Player (who you met previously) is an Amplifier. They know everyone. Examples of Amplifiers would be recruiters, business development or sales people; they are old hands at networking and get the reciprocal nature of how networking works. Amplifiers are your advocates. They like you, they sell you, and they run interference on your behalf.

You definitely need to create opportunities to build Amplifiers into your networking plan. But you can't just rely on them because they don't know your ultimate career goal, so you need some skin in the game yourself.

Your (future) Sector is when you start connecting with people already in the direction/sector/industry/level where you are heading. Once again, if you don't know where you are going, how will you know when you get there? Work it out so you can start proactively building out your networks in that direction. This could be as easy as connecting with people, via LinkedIn, in a particular organisation for which you want to work. It could also mean going to industry events in a new sector even though you're not there yet or learning more by getting industry publications and connecting with thinkers and leaders in that sector. Make success a fait accompli by getting connected before you get there.

Finally, ensure your plan includes meeting **Decision Makers.** Decision Makers will be different for different people. In some cases, it will be your boss or your boss's boss. This may take more effort and creativity but it's a powerful tactic. This means you must go where Decision Makers go, hang out where Decision Makers hang out—as they are less likely to come to you. Or if you are super smart, create opportunities for Decision Makers to come to you by offering them something like a panel opportunity, a writing opportunity or an opportunity to address your advisory committee or board.

For many years, as part of my own networking strategy, I would identify organisations that ran events that attracted Decision Makers and simply go their quarterly meetups. One particular event was the American Chamber of Commerce breakfast and the CEO Forum for Association Professionals where I knew that I would be seated with peers or those with influence. At the time I was busy running a peak body, so these were the only networking events I attended.

This approach worked so well for me; I landed two roles over the course of my career as a result of getting out of my comfort zone and going to events to meet decision makers.

What's next?

You need to make a plan. This plan combines visibility opportunities (where you are seen and heard) and networking (where you are seen, heard and valued). Remember, whatever plan you execute is better than the one that sits in the cupboard.

Activity

The following pages display an annual plan. It has quarterly activities aligned with your newly defined brand as identified in Chapter 4 and linked to your longer term career goals. You can do this for yourself as well.

- Grab an A3 page and turn to landscape.
- Divide the page into quarters as per the following example.
- Each quarter, plan the sorts of networking and visibility activities you need to do in three categories: internal (inside your organisation), external (to industry more broadly) and online forums.
- Complete your plan for the year setting up quarterly and annual activities. Note: I've completed a plan for you below as an example. There is no problem with leaving a space blank. Remember, progress is better than perfect. Strategic is better than busy. The plan that you do is better than the plan that sits on the shelf and you don't do.

	Q1	Q2	Q3	Q4
	Internal	Internal	Internal	Internal
Low Hanging Fruit	Ad hoc staff networking functions	Ad hoc management function	Ad hoc staff networking functions	Ad hoc management Xmas drinks
Amplifiers	Lunch meeting with peers who are happy to champion me	Repeat Q2	Repeat Q3	Repeat Q4
Future Direction	Monthly coffee meeting with three different managers at one level higher to ask about their division	Repeat Q2	Repeat Q3	Repeat Q4
Decision Makers	Create/find opportunities to present a report to the C-suite executives	Put your hand up for an initiative that will go to the board for approval	Invite the CEO to contribute to the panel you are putting together	Offer to interview the MD for the all staff broadcast news
	External	External	External	External
Low Hanging Fruit	Accepting any invitation that comes your way—possibly mostly women's only networking events	Repeat	Repeat	Repeat
Amplifiers	Quarterly meeting with your industry sponsor and vendor partner	Speak at industry conference	Get published/featured in industry magazine or be interviewed for an industry publication	Get yourself on a panel for an industry conference
Future Direction	Attend seminar in future direction	Consider stakeholders, clients, customers		

	Q1	Q2	Q3	Q4
Decision Makers	Choose an activity outside of work where you will more likely meet decision makers*	Weekly cycling with the partners	Attend CEO forum conference	Attend CEO forum Xmas function
	Online	Online	Online	Online
Low Hanging Fruit	Weekly schedule of liking things in your feed and connecting and commenting on what comes your way or that LinkedIn suggests	Repeat Q2	Repeat Q3	Repeat Q4
Amplifiers	Weekly appointment to connect with one recruiter or influencer and/or comment on a post by an influencer or an influencer in your industry	Repeat	Repeat	Repeat
Future Direction	Connect and comment on influencers and others on LinkedIn in your future direction	Repeat	Share content from other people that interests you	Repeat
Decision Makers	Monthly curation or creation of a leadership LinkedIn post or article, then sending it to key Decision Makers in your network to comment	Repeat	Repeat	Repeat

*It doesn't have to be work related. Here in Australia, cycling is popular. Female cyclists are always telling me how good their cycling has been to their career as they get to mingle with managing partners and others at more senior levels in their careers. Cycling is definitely the new golf.

PART 3

CHAPTER 7

TACTICS TO TRY IN AND AROUND THE OFFICE

Be pitch ready

There are elevator pitches and there are elevator pitches. There is the old school pitch where you get to speak as fast as you can for a minute or two as the elevator moves. This pitch is well past its 'best by' date. Luckily, there is a new pitch that's designed to entice, engage and open up the conversation far more effectively.

The *Gaddie Pitch* (thanks Antony Gaddie) addresses:

- The problems you solve
- The difference you make
- The value you add.

It's also a great way to get a humble brag in. Not something needy or overly self-deprecating but a sincere, factual, evidence-based conversation with a real result. It goes like this:

- You know when … (describe a problem with which the recipient might identify, and that you solve).
- Well what I do … (three broad brush things you bring to help solve the problem; don't be too technical).
- Most recently, I was working with … and I did this … and I delivered …. (Quantify and/or qualify.)

Don't worry if people interrupt you. It's a conversation starter and an invitation to engage further. If someone does interrupt, see if you can get it back on track but don't be overly dogmatic about it. Instead, try your pitches where you are less likely to be interrupted. Examples include:

- When asked to introduce yourself in meetings, remember you are far more interesting than just a job title (help others see you in a different light).
- When presenting from the stage, why not weave in a pitch in the first five minutes or as your intro for a panel discussion?
- At networking functions, keep it punchy and conversational.
- On teleconferencing, well, you'll wow them too.

Don't get too stuck on the exact wording of your pitch. Play around with the formula until the language matches your style. For example, 'you now when' could be replaced with:

- Imagine when
- Picture this
- Have you ever experienced ..... ?

The benefits of this style of elevator pitch? Whenever you get to provide an example, this grounds your pitch in context, fact and substance. It boosts your credibility and keeps it real. (Refer to the Friday Formula in *Intranet and other internal ideas*).

Below are two of my own examples. But just so you know, I have five or six depending on the audience and situation.

Example 1:

Imagine this ... you're a deep subject matter expert. You're great at solving complex nuanced business problems requiring strategy, operations and emotional intelligence. But instead of getting the promotion, the pay rise or the better opportunity, you get another messy problem to solve.

I help with ... tactics, strategy and branding tools, so that you never feel stuck again.

Just last month ... I was working with a woman who was deeply unhappy in her role; she had unfortunately jumped from the frying pan into the fire with a rapid job change that hadn't worked out. She could feel sorry for herself or do something about it. She chose to do something about it. She put herself forward for a prestigious award (and won!). This grew her confidence, so she resigned and in just two months, she landed an even better role in a company where she knows she will excel—it also came with a 30% increase in pay.

Example 2:

You know when ... you've spent your entire career looking after everyone else, but forgotten to do the same for yourself?

Well what I do ... is provide a fresh approach to tackling 'brand you' that will halve your time and double your impact.

In fact, just this month ... I helped a woman pitch well above the perception of her capability. Her boss resigned in a rush and she rang me because she wanted a plan to step into the breach. Together, we crafted something she felt comfortable and confident to pitch to the CEO. We rehearsed language and reframes that would keep her on the front foot and playing big. She not only landed her boss's job but went on to negotiate a $90k+ increase in salary.

Activity

Executive women: prepare yourself two elevator pitches. One for internal purposes (inside your organisation) and the other for external purpose (when you meet customers, stakeholders or clients).

Consultants: prepare yourself two or three elevator pitches. All pitches should be designed around:

The work you are currently doing.
The work you want to be doing more of in the future (more engaging, more lucrative, more sustainable).
Other projects or client bases where you want to be doing more work.

Become your own marketing department

Help others to help you

Your boss is busy; they are the protagonist in their own movie after all. Make it easy for them and tell them about your wins, achievements, what you are currently working on and your aspirations. Don't be shy about these things. Next time your boss or a member of the leadership team asks what you are working on, don't demur and dismiss it or provide a 'nothing' answer. Instead, think of it as an elevator pitch opportunity.

Why not share about a piece of work you are doing that excites you? Keep it succinct and offer the opportunity for the listener to learn more at a later date, but do take advantage of this opportunity. Or, why not share about a result you just delivered? Especially, if it's a good news story. Too many of us might reply with 'oh nothing much'.

Don't be a creator of your own flat, boring and drawn out career journey. Instead, be the creator of your exciting career adventure.

 Case study

Jade had a particular area of expertise that was in high demand at a large bank. She liked working at the bank. She felt loyal to the bank but wanted to develop and stretch in other ways. The enterprise had several social justice venture partnerships in play and Jade was interested in one of the NFP organisations. She played an active role in volunteering in her somewhat scant spare time.

Suddenly the NFP needed a new CEO and Jade was able (after negotiation with her boss and a champion) to throw her hat in the ring to be considered as a secondment placement. She won the role, performed in it for a year, and then went back to her regular role inside the bank.

What had she learned? She got direct P&L responsibility, leadership experience, governance, and risk and compliance experience. Plus, she got to deliver on more direct outcomes that weren't always available to her inside a large enterprise. The experience and skills she learned are significant assets on her resume, which she can leverage in the future.

Create a distribution plan

Why not have a distribution plan to share key wins, achievements and progress? Think about those who may be interested or invested in your success and future. Add to that those who may be influential in your career journey and success. Then make a plan to share with them strategically and periodically about your journey. Keep them informed, just like managing upwards—proactively, strategically and deliberately.

My theory is that everyone is busy with their own career journey. So, make it easy for others to help you by giving them information and ammunition that helps them see what you've done and where you'd be useful in the future. We all like to back a winner. If you are genuinely doing great work and sincere about your future aspirations, others will be happy to help you.

Don't keep your plans a secret

Make sure your boss and possibly even your boss's boss, know about your potential plans within the company. Don't keep it a secret or you'll be the one who is disappointed. Do focus on the job at hand, but don't be shy about developing and sharing a career development plan inside the organisation that has your future career aspirations in mind.

 Case study

I work with a smart 'n' savvy executive women, named Eli, who is incredibly proactive in this way. In fact, she takes it to the next level. By the time she started in a new role she had already done the following:

- Updated her resume with details of her new role and the three key KPIs as discussed with her at interview.
- Gone back out to people who had helped her in the recruitment phase:
  - » to thank them for their help
  - » to provide them with the updated version of her resume
  - » to suggest that she would get back in touch in a year to update them again, but likely wouldn't be on the market again for another two years. ('However, do get in touch if something eminently suitable comes up.')

- Been clear with her new manager about her career aspirations (ostensibly with this new organisation) and asked for help on how she could get there. In one instance, she had had an open conversation with her manager about one day having a role like theirs and asked for their advice on achieving this. Her new manager didn't see her as a threat but put together a development plan spanning three years to help her achieve the role or one just like it.

This was all within the first month of starting her new role. It's not disloyal, over-confident or a waste of time. It's future-focused, deliberate, ambitious and highly effective.

Keep a compliments folder

If you don't have a compliments or an applause folder, then you are simply shooting yourself in the foot. This is a must-have for any professional. It's useful in a wide range of circumstances including:

- When you are feeling blue and need a boost of confidence or are fending off a case of Imposter Syndrome.
- When preparing for performance appraisals.
- When preparing for salary discussions.
- When nominating for awards.
- When applying for roles.
- When updating your resume or LinkedIn profile.

I suggest making it electronic so you can take it anywhere, but don't make the mistake of thinking that if it's on the work server, it belongs to you. In fact, it doesn't. Make sure you have a personal copy that does not sit on the work server. I've heard of several bad news stories of personal files being lost when kept on the work server including:

- Someone being 'walked' with no warning, so had no opportunity to collect that evidence.
- An email lock out pending some sort of investigation.

Bad things can happen to good people despite the best of intentions and in an increasingly litigious world, you want to make sure you are smart about looking after yourself and your compliments folder. The moral of this story, is keep your compliments folder on your own personal device.

 (Winning) Case study

Carla, a wonderful client, was feeling overwhelmed as she prepared to go on holiday. It had been a big year. It was at the end of financial year and mid-winter here in Australia. She suggested she would mothball nominating for an award until the following year, even though it had been on her 12-month plan. Others around her were all in agreement because it was true. She was worn out.

You can imagine my response.

There had to be a smarter way. Old thinking such as *working hard, brand busy and relentless execution* will only get you so far and will keep you worn out.

What about a new and easier way of tackling this? After devising a new strategy for tackling the award that included hiring an award nomination writer, she was not only *effortlessly* nominated for one award, but found another award opportunity while she was away. She felt so good about herself after the process that she created two more award nomination opportunities upon her return.

Even better, her award nomination efforts were successful. She was named winner in the *2018 Greater Brisbane Business Woman of the Year Award.* When asked how she did it? She said 'Remember my compliments folder? I've been diligent in documenting wins, achievements and keeping compliments. I simply handed my folder to the nomination writer before I left. And it all went from there'.

If that's not a good argument for keeping neat and organised records of wins, achievements and compliments, I don't know what is. She achieved all this while lying poolside on a *drop and flop* holiday.

Create champions, advocates and amplifiers in high places

Remember Figure 6 (the *Power up your networking* model)? There is a section dedicated to creating amplifiers? This is going to be so integral to your success that I want to re-emphasise. If you want to lead and succeed and are invested in your career, you need to create champions, advocates and amplifiers with access to high places. It's not enough to have a cheer squad of peers, staff or supportive friends and family members. You also need a high level cheer squad to run interference, sing your praises, provide introductions, put you forward and smooth your way in the more senior levels of your organisation or industry.

Why? Because when you aren't there to defend yourself, these people will have your back. When an ideal opportunity (for you) presents itself, these people will put you forward. When someone makes a suggestion that's going to create friction for your division, they will not only put your case forward, but also give you a heads up so you can do something about it. In the rarefied air of the C-suite, sometimes decisions are made about you without you being in the room. You want high level people on your side.

How? Invest now. Invest in creating positive connections with people above you on the org chart. Help them to help you by being able to share the value of your work and how you add impact. Keep them up to date about key initiatives, and offer to assist them as they need.

Research proves time and time again that one of the biggest roadblocks for women at senior levels is the lack of senior level champions and sponsors. There is an opportunity for you to proactively and pre-emptively put a plan in place now.

Intranet and other internal ideas

Treat the intranet like LinkedIn

The company intranet is a great way to build your brand and become known beyond your division. Don't underestimate it. If your company doesn't have an intranet, maybe there is an all-staff email newsletter. Either way, from now on, you are going to be an active contributor. Building your brand on the intranet is just like building your brand on LinkedIn. Work out what you want to be known for: Is it as someone who is nice and helpful? Is it as someone who cleans up after everyone else? Or is it as the person who knows how to voice their opinion or how to drive collaboration or deliver big results?

Second, work out where you want to be professionally in six months, a year or two years. It doesn't have to be locked in stone, but *do* have some direction or goal. Then start collecting and documenting topics that are in alignment with your goals and brand, so they can be shared. I suggest creating a schedule for sharing these topics. It could be as complicated as three shares per week:

- Monday: a motivational upbeat theme; let's do great things this week together.
- Wednesday: a technical expertise article or leadership article share.
- Friday: something a little lighter like a GoalCast video.

Key things to remember:

- Don't overdo it. Too much sharing is almost, but not quite, as bad as not doing anything at all.
- Keep it professional. The intranet is *not* Facebook.
- Keep it in alignment with your goals.

Other internal tactics

- Offer to run or host an internal 'lunch and learn' activity to share insights about various individuals' or departments' work. This is great for breaking down silos.
- Offer to do a 10-min presentation, at another division's staff meeting, to share your expertise on a particular issue where cross-pollination might be helpful.
- Schedule 2–3 coffee meetings per month outside your division with other influencers or stakeholders with whom you are not (yet) working.
- Send articles of interest to others who may be important to your career journey. This will demonstrate that you are thinking broadly: 'Here's an article on what we spoke about yesterday. Given your perspective on XYZ, I thought you'd find it useful'.

Dress like the SHEO

Dress for the job you want, not for the job you have—even on casual Friday. Internal promotions rarely happen as the result of an interview, despite what you imagine. In a world that is increasingly focused on appearance and personal branding, your image counts just as much as your impact. Trivial but true. Dressing professionally indicates you take yourself and your career seriously. It demonstrates respect for your work environment, your craft or expertise, the people you work with and yourself. It shows that you are professional and that you value your own contribution.

Does this mean wearing exclusive labels to work every day? No. But it does mean elevating your standards so your future aspirations and your current self, intersect easily.

The Friday Formula

Given that most of us have a negativity bias (for example, we remember what went wrong, rather than what went right), the Friday Formula is especially useful.

Every Friday you must document/journal the following:

- What you achieved that week? (personal or professional)
- The benefit you delivered (financial or otherwise, quantify or qualify)
- The core skill/expertise used to deliver that achievement.

Author and self-promotion guru Peggy Klaus, suggests starting a *bragalogue*. I love this idea. The above formula will help you collect evidence that is factual, contextual and backed up enough to pre-emptively bank credibility.

If you establish this sort of habit, it stands you in great stead for those times when:

- someone pushes back on you in a meeting and you begin to doubt yourself.
- you are feeling blue or worn out.
- you need to proactively self-promote
- you can feel a case of Imposter Syndrome creeping in and you want to nip it in the bud.

Realistic optimism is far more effortlessly maintained when you have the evidence. It is a great antidote to negativity bias and Imposter Syndrome.

Meetings and ad hoc corridor chats

Various studies have documented that the casual corridor chat is far from a waste of time. According to one study, while an estimated 25–70% of work time is spent in face-to-face interactions, 30% consists of casual conversations. Another study found that people were less productive and less able to carry out their jobs when casual conversations were not possible.

So why not be prepared? If you've done the pre-work: you've created a visibility strategy and a networking plan, plus you have your career strategy roughly mapped out, then you are perfectly poised to take advantage of those 'out of the blue' moments or meetings that might come your way.

If you are *lucky* and someone takes the time to ask what you want for your next role, respond clearly. Do not say 'Oh, I'm not really sure' in an attempt to hedge your bets. Make it easy for others to help you by having a pre-prepared framework with three verbal bullet points about what you'd like to be doing in the future.

Here are two examples of this framework in action in response to 'what's your ideal role?'

I'm looking for my next level project leadership role. Ideally it would be:

- collaborative in nature
- in engineering
- would enable me to leverage my client/stakeholder relationship expertise.

I'm looking for my next challenge in (insert company/industry/field here). Ideally it would include:

- people leadership
- looking at future trends
- with customer at the core.

Hedging your bets or trying to be all things to all people confuses the issue and makes you seem wishy-washy. Own and claim your expertise then reap the rewards. Being visible, along with being able to capitalise on that visibility, is more powerful. Don't hang back.

 Activity

Create a possible framework for your next ideal role. Practice it out loud with a friend or peer to see what it sounds like and to make sure you're not pitching too low. Get feedback, revise if required and try it out next time someone asks you what you might be looking for. Even better, don't wait for someone to ask; instead, create an opportunity to try it out with a Decision Maker or Amplifier with whom you have contact. Remember, this framework can flex and change as you grow or your goals change. It's a framework, not a pigeon hole. Use it as such.

Peer promotion, cohorts and coalitions

'Build selective enduring relationships with others in your field and collaborate for mutual promotion.'

—Brenda Knowles

Peer promotion: the executive woman's best friend

Ever noticed how much easier it is to use superlatives, or say great things about your best friend? Yet if someone pays you a compliment, you're more likely to deflect or be self-deprecating? This is why peer promotion works particularly well for women. It's where you get someone else to say great things about you because you are uncomfortable saying it yourself or you are worried about being criticised.

I like peer promotion for its three-fold benefit:

1. Your friend or peer is likely to use more powerful words about you than you would use yourself.

2. You may start believing the words your friend or peer is saying.

3. You don't even need to be there. It might be a meeting you don't want to attend, but you peer has your back: 'Hey, Jane is great at dispute resolution. In fact, she's *the* industry expert. You should invite her to be on this Task Force. Shall I let her know?'

You can be systematic about it too. You could buddy up with a peer or office friend and ensure you each put each other forward for opportunities. And the best bit? You can include men in this as well. After all, with men still holding more than 80% of leadership roles, you can't afford not to include them, so don't limit yourself to female peers. You could even take turns to write about and highlight each other's achievement(s) on the intranet or in some internal publication.

Every now and then, when I talk about peer promotion, someone will ask about women competing and comparing each other. If this is an issue for you, simply partner with peers who are aligned but don't compete. Don't throw the baby out with the bathwater because someone competed with you once for a role or opportunity.

 Case study

I work with a stylist, Julie Hyne. Julie is great. She truly understands how our deep-seated concerns about body shape and image, along with standing out to fit in, can undermine our best attempts at breaking through the glass ceiling. She calls herself The Style Whisperer, but when I introduce Julie I introduce her as the CEO stylist. Julie wouldn't call herself this because she feels embarrassed.

Julie works with many CEOs and managing directors around Australia; therefore, I am simply stating a fact, plus it gives my brand a credibility boost. But for Julie to say that about herself makes her uncomfortable. Thankfully, she is happy for me to do it.

Having someone else say good things about you is far easier than you saying them yourself. Develop a peer support network with non-competing peers and create ways to peer promote.

Cohorts and coalitions

This strategy also dovetails nicely into the coalitions and cohorts approach, where women support each other's *voice* openly in meetings. Remember, most of us want to be seen, heard AND valued, yet the challenge remains that women are frequently spoken over and their perspective lost.

You may have heard of the following terms:

- *Bro-propration:* where a man appropriates your idea deliberately or inadvertently.

- *Manterruptions:* where a man interrupts and speaks over you. In a 2014 study out of the tech industry, men were found twice as likely to interrupt others and three times as likely to interrupt a woman.
- *Mansplaining:* where a man explains something in which you are the expert. It's as though their opinion is worth more. Often, they don't know they're doing it—it's ingrained socially for them.
- *Manspreading:* where men are simply more comfortable taking up more space. Women are socialised to be small, dainty and diminutive, while the stereotype for a strong male is large and dominating. Donald Trump, US President, is frequently seen clearing the table in front of him when he sits down at a table to haggle. Manspreading is a tactic you might try yourself.
- I'd like to add *Manopolising* to this list. This is where men monopolise the airtime at the office, in meetings or in other places where professional conversations occur.

Former Australian Foreign Minister and Deputy Prime Minister, Julie Bishop MP, made the press in October of 2017 when she spoke at the *Women's Weekly Women of the Future* event in Sydney about being not heard. Bishop described the approach of her fellow cabinet members as a kind of unconscious bias, 'almost a deafness' to her contribution. She went on to share that once several more women were appointed to cabinet, she joined forces with the other women and made use of this *cohort and coalition tactic*. In order to ensure the female voice and perspective remained heard, her female colleagues supported each other. When one made a point, the others would all agree or reinforce the point in the background with comments like 'Well done Julie, great perspective, let's hear more of this'. If Julie or one of the other women was interrupted mid-sentence, they had a pact to call it out.

> *'They became far more powerful together
> than they ever could have been alone.'*
>
> — Jamila Rizvi, author of *Not Just Lucky*

What can we do? We can do the same in meetings with our peers and in environments where only the loudest and most confident get the airtime and where diverse perspectives are brushed over. Form a coalition of sorts to back each other's contributions to ensure all contributions are heard and new ideas from women are equally considered. While this is not strictly self-promotion, being an active contributor, whose ideas and opinions are heard and considered (and attributed to you) is a good initial step.

 Activity

Identify potential peer promotors. Who could you buddy up with to champion you, spruik you up, inside or outside the office?

Putting your hand up for plum assignments

Putting your hand up for plum assignments is a great way to get noticed. Look for assignments that are slightly out of your comfort zone. Choose ones that give you more visibility with Decision Makers or movers and shakers within the business or industry, or where you think the results will look great on your resume. This means:

- Not hanging back and imagining that someone else might be more worthy because they are better or have been in the department longer than you.
- Not simply hoping that opportunities might find you. You have to keep asking, influencing and demonstrating your willingness.

- Letting go of old beliefs about whether you are skilled at something or not. You can learn. Start backing your ability to learn and upskill fast; this will be one of the single most valuable currencies in your career. (We are seeing unprecedented change in the skills and expertise required at work in future years.)

- Stop waiting until you feel ready. Those people kicking goals have learned to launch well before they *feel* ready. Feeling and being ready are two different beasts. Stop confusing them.

- Stop waiting for your annual performance appraisal to ask for what you want. Ask, influence and demonstrate interest year round. On that note and slightly off topic, stop waiting for the salary review time to initiate a salary discussion with your boss and talk about the value you have added. Go early and go often. The early bird catches the worm. Your results and your salary expectations won't be a surprise if you've been feeding your boss information along the way.

- Stop waiting to be invited. Invite yourself. If you don't have a seat at the table, BYO chair.

- Be prepared to respond to the 'why you' question. Once again, don't wait to be asked. Give them the evidence beforehand. If you've been doing your Friday Formula, this should be easy.

 Case study

Recently, as part of her work, Lisa got to go to the UN. Where previously she might have hesitated to put her hand up and ask for the gig, she decided she had nothing to lose by asking, so she did. And was successful. It was as simple as that.

Activity

What opportunities, offered by your organisation, would you like to get involved in?

Can you get involved with a division that carries out work, where there might be a cross functional component? For example, an advisory committee or collaborative project component?

Is there a gap in your resume that you want to fill? Can you fill those gaps with an assignment or secondment placement?

In there an opportunity to create these in your current work environment? What about your peak body/professional association? Does your organisation offer opportunities to do charity or NFP work?

Start mapping out what you need to do differently in order to start taking advantage of plum assignments or opportunities that light your fire.

Shifting from passive to proactive and Rockstar self-promotion

'I am smart, I am talented, I take advantage of the opportunities that come my way and I work really, really hard. Don't call me lucky. Call me a badass.'

—Shonda Rhimes

There is a saying that luck is what happens when preparation meets opportunity. Right now, you want to get lucky in advance. Those who are truly going places, have different habits and mindset than the rest. They don't wait to be discovered or rescued or until they are in desperate need. Instead, they create their own reality early and often, so that it appears they are lucky when someone invites them to interview for their dream role.

Imagine what could happen if you actually tried?

Remember how many young girls have been and still are socialised to have less agency? This means, that in the background, they are running a script that downplays the need to take more assertive action or voices that assertive action is wrong. In fact, Michele Meyer-Shipp, KPMG's Chief Diversity Officer says 'This tendency – to focus on behaviours that are task-oriented over those that are self-assertive – is a pattern that repeats itself throughout the survey findings'. (KPMG, 2019)

When women start working with me, there is usually a moment when we laugh about the opportunities they are now effortlessly creating. They say 'imagine what would happen if I actually tried?' What might be possible if you actually laid out a career strategy in alignment with your sense of purpose? One with a tactical self-promotion plan to back it up? One that you review every month, with some accountability, progress measures and some big hairy audacious goals built in? Is it possible that instead of feeling like you're not seen, heard or valued, you might in fact be surprised at how much you can achieve?

Here are some examples on shifting from passive to proactive to Rockstar self-promotion tactics. They will give you some ideas about what else you might be doing if you actually put your mind to it. Once you've worked out the formula, have a play with some of the self-promotion activities you regularly do (or think you should do), and see how you might take them to the next level so you end up doing Rockstar self-promotion activities with ease.

Passive	Reactive	Proactive	Rockstar self-promotion
Reading articles on LinkedIn	Responding and commenting to articles	Sharing articles	Curating and sharing themed content consistently, over a period of time, in alignment with your strategic objective and future brand. Invite people who are key to your success to contribute to the discussion.
Liking other people's published content on LinkedIn	Commenting on other people's published content	Publishing your own content	Publishing themed content over a period of time in alignment with your strategic goals and future brand, then distributing to key stakeholders or other experts for commentary. Once again include any people key to your future success to contribute to the discussion as well.
Not connecting (and being suspicious of every connection request) on LinkedIn	Waiting for people to connect with you then accepting	Sending out connections randomly or when you remember to	Systematically and routinely growing connections in the direction of your choice and following up with a breezy yet branded message and offering to help if needed. Maybe scheduling a 10-minute phone call to get to know each other better.
Not responding to or not sending messages on LinkedIn	Using LinkedIn preprogrammed messages in response	Initiating and responding with tailored messages	Programmed, themed and strategic messaging plan to drive engagement and connection. 1. after connection 2. after a month 3. after three months.
Simply completing the basics of your LinkedIn with job titles and companies	Updating your LinkedIn profile only after someone sends you a note that your profile is out of date or after you've landed a new role	Actively updating your profile ensuring searchability and functionality as your career evolves or before you start looking for a new role or opportunity	Strategically and thematically updating your profile to help position you in a new or different way in a new market or to springboard into a promotion or a new direction and creating content that reinforces your career strategy.

Passive	Reactive	Proactive	Rockstar self-promotion
Waiting to be discovered or waiting until you are past your use-by date in your current role and applying, in a rush, when it's urgent or an emergency	Applying for roles you find or see on LinkedIn or other	Proactively reaching out to your network and recruiters to let them know you are in the market for a new role when the time comes	Proactively (and in advance) running a strategic and scheduled campaign based around your future career aspirations, so that roles come to you. Updating your LinkedIn profile and resume every six months and proactively sending to recruiters to update their file and keep in touch. Reaching out to your network every 3–6 months to share ideas on what's happening in the market, and what opportunities will be on the horizon. Focus on • the problems you solve • the difference you make • the value you add. All with a focus on you, your future and an underlying theme of reciprocity (give and take)
Know about awards and go along to them, talk about nominating one day but don't bother	Wait for someone to nominate you for an award and when they do, you throw your hat in the ring	Actively seek out awards to nominate for and submit nominations	Put a 3-year plan in place in alignment with your career goals that include award recognition. Research the best awards for your sector and also the ones that will either deliver the best ROI (prestigious) or are perhaps easier to win. Work out what the application process is and how to fill any gaps in experience that may be needed to become noticed by the award. Regularly collect evidence and data in support. Employ a 3rd party to help you write or edit your award nomination because it's really challenging to write glowing things about yourself when you tend to underestimate your own achievements. Have a plan in place for if/when you are named finalist or winner to be able to leverage the opportunity; acceptance speech, social media, communication and media plan.

Activity

Identify something you might do that could be good for your career. Unpack the activity, as I have above, into four columns from Passive to Rockstar self-promotion. Notice how easy the Proactive or Rockstar categories appear when you write them down this way. The proof is in the pudding and you need to execute. Lock these activities in your diary and make a date with yourself to execute. Identify something you might do that could be good for your career. Unpack the activity, as I have above, into four columns from Passive to Rockstar self-promotion. Notice how easy the Proactive or Rockstar categories appear when you write them down this way. The proof of the pudding is in the eating, and you need to execute. Lock these activities in your diary and make a date with yourself to execute.

CHAPTER 8

EXTERNAL SELF-PROMOTION IDEAS (ACTIVITIES AND IDEAS OUTSIDE OF YOUR CURRENT ORGANISATION)

Are women's conferences worth it?

Shawn Achor seems to think so.

(Vested interest: I'm in the airport Lounge waiting to head up the Gartner Senior Women in Multinationals Retreat).

Back to Shawn. He was so challenged by the scepticism displayed by a fellow plane passenger that he decided to conduct some research to test the theory. This is what he discovered:

In the year after connecting with peers at the Conference for Women the likelihood of receiving a promotion doubled.
In one year, attendees had triple the likelihood of a 10%+ pay increase.
78% percent of attendees reported feeling 'more optimistic about the future'.

Other critical determiners from his own observations of 900 conferences included:

- A sense of social connection felt by the attendees.
- Engaging sessions.

- Leaders who role model and exemplify the qualities that the conference is attempting to instil.
- A memorable moment.
- A realistic assessment of the present with an optimistic look to the future.

My take? Put a few conferences designed for women into your networking mix—men included. Many of the stories and case studies are inspiring in their own right, and they might just lead to winning that pay rise, promotion or recognition you truly deserve.

Attending conferences, even if you're not a speaker

The best networkers I know go to a conference with a plan. First, they select their conferences wisely—they are in alignment with their future goals. Consider who will be in the audience, on the speaker panel or in the delegation whom you might want to get in front of.

If you do end up at some random conference, you can still make it pay off. Before the conference, connect with the speakers via LinkedIn and remember to personalise your connection request. It can be something like *I see you're speaking at the XYZ conference. I'll be there too and am really looking forward to your session. Good luck! Let's connect on LinkedIn. It looks like a great program.* Note the tone is breezy, not cheesy or sleazy. So important.

Do your research before the conference and identify three or four key speakers whom you want to get to know better professionally. Perhaps their topic resonates or is in the direction you want to go. If they connect with you on LinkedIn, send another message to your hit list of three or four and suggest that if they are going to be around you'd love to say hi and interview them for your blog. Be really clear here. Many of the speakers are speaking for free and do so because they may win customers or clients. Their break times, during conferences, are important, so don't try and hog that time unless you have serious intentions of being a customer down the track.

Make yourself known. It's a lonely business, speaking at a conference, particularly if there is another speaker immediately following. You can feel a little abandoned and unloved. Having someone come up immediately following your session, saying hi and thanking you for your speech etc. is really quite fabulous. Don't be shy. This also makes you more memorable, so when you both have more time you could potentially hit them up for a coffee to ask advice or gain insights.

Other tactics as an attendee

- Take a photo of a slide of one of the key presenters or create a photo collage of a few. Create a LinkedIn post and tag the speakers. Timing is everything. The biggest mistake I see here is people finishing their post at 8 pm, after the conference dinner or cocktail party finishes. No-one is on LinkedIn at that time; you'll get a better result if you wait until the next morning or lunchtime.
- Grab a photo with one of the speakers (again, be considerate of timing). Can you get an action shot rather than one of you posing for the camera?
- Create a summary article with notes and key learnings from the conference. Publish it on LinkedIn, or on your company intranet at the end of the event. This could be modified as a report for your team.
- Create a mini video blog at the end of each day and distribute via LinkedIn. What are your thoughts? How will this event help you?

- Interview a few people at the conference via video. Be sure to get their permission to publish.

 Case study

Back in the early days of Twitter, one of my very proactive SOCAP Australia members would curate key Tweets from each of our conferences to make up a report. He'd send it to us and we'd then circulate it to our members; however, he would get all the credit because his name and Twitter handle were plastered across the top. We even gave him special mentions in the program and made sure to thank him publicly at each event because he was being incredibly helpful and providing great value. Remember, curating and making meaning out of information is a really cool self-promotion tool. Don't underestimate it.

Networking tips for those who truly hate networking

'Learn to love networking.'

—Catriona Pollard

Yes, you *do* need to network. I know you hate it, but networking does help. And with a plan, you can make it fun and turn it into a challenge.

Here are three tips to help you shift from the Fixer mode (strategic but low visibility) to the Rockstar (high visibility plus strategic) within a few months. Instead of going along to ad hoc, random events resentfully, I suggest treating them like any other project at work.

1. Strategically plan the events you go to at the beginning of the year and make sure you include mixed gender networking events.

Successful men and women plan their event schedule 12 months in advance. Really? Yes really. It's smart, less reactive, and you're committed. By creating a plan of one strategic event per month, you are playing 'above the line'. Below the line, there are excuses, blame, resentment, avoidance and not accepting responsibility for your own part in the process. Above the line, you are accepting responsibility and creating your own career success and reality: *Step Up, Speak Out and Take Charge.*

- Most peak bodies and industry groups organise their calendars in the latter part of the year. If you work for a large corporate, it is wise to be seen at the internal corporate events. Review the events schedule, make a plan in advance and book them in well ahead of time. Of course, ad-hoc events will come up, and you will always have a choice.

- If you do work for a large corporate, it can be tempting to only network within your organisation. While loyalty is admired by some, the smarter play is to also network externally. Once again, get out of your comfort zone and put external networking in your plan.

- Remember the criteria of the 'right audience'? You need to be seen and heard by the Decision Makers and leaders of your industry and/or business. Rule of thumb: until such time as we have more than 19% women in senior leadership roles, you will definitely need to attend mixed gender networking events to ensure you are noticed by the right people in positions of power. However, in the initial stages of your career, women's only events can be great for confidence building and meeting like-minded professionals. However, until we see more women in leadership roles, create a program that includes both women's only events and mixed gender events.

2. Advance preparation before attending networking events

- **Connect with the speaker in advance** with a short note saying you are looking forward to hearing them speak at the event. Maybe offer to introduce them to your connections, or comment on an article they've written. This will make you stand out.

- **Connect with the organiser in advance** (LinkedIn, Twitter and/or email). Write a short note about how much you are looking forward to the event and offer to help with introductions or prepping questions from the floor: *By the way, here's an article I wrote on the topic. It might be useful for audience questions.* (No pressure!). As with most panel discussions or seminars, the wise event planner sets up a few audience members with questions. This could be your chance to stand out and be noticed. Why not volunteer to be one of the seeds?

- **Create an action plan**. It doesn't have to be complicated. My plan is always to walk away with five new connections— either business cards or LinkedIn connections. Note: it's easy to connect on LinkedIn then and there. Otherwise make a note on the business card then scan. I use the app, Cam Card. I also plan some questions in case the conversation dries up. Reflect on open questions that get the other person talking about themselves comfortably and easily. Talk about their role, the problems they solve, the difference they make, the value they add, their organisation, the future of the industry, opportunities in industry, new developments, other industry events etc.

- **Be pitch ready.** Have your elevator pitch prepared in advance. Let's face it, job titles are boring and so subjective. Plus, you are far more than the sum of those three or four words on your business card. Unless your job title is something like *Catalyst for Magic,* then an elevator pitch is far more helpful.
- **Prepare to ask questions from the back of the room.** Do your homework and prep them in advance. This is part of the *Step Up, Speak Out, Take Charge* process. You need to develop a voice that can be heard and is valued, so prepare and rehearse. One of the smartest women I know does this on a regular basis. She has a PhD and is naturally a little shy. But she always sounds extremely confident when asking questions from the floor. I puzzled over this for months, until I asked for her secret: preparation—she nearly always prepares a question in advance.

3. At the networking event

- **Invite a 'wing woman'.** I try to take a peer or client to networking events. We introduce each other to various people we meet. This doubles your chances of meeting the right people at the right time and eliminates the need to tell people how awesome you are because someone else will do it for you. Hold each other accountable and turn it into a game. Can you each find five people who would be ideal to introduce to each other? Then it becomes less about you and more about them.
- **Say hello and/or thanks to the speaker at the event.** Speakers love to connect with the audience and usually crave some sort of feedback. As mentioned, it's a lonely and vulnerable job out the front, and even if you didn't like everything they said, speakers appreciate an in-person

'thanks'. After all, they're just like you but are a little further on their journey.

- **Ditto with the organiser**. Make sure the organiser knows who you are, what you stand for, and that you are open to being introduced. Okay, so they may be busy on the day, but they will be extremely well connected, and part of their job will be to introduce people, so make it easy for them to help you.

- **Be sure to speak to senior leaders at the event** and so you don't feel stupid or shy, mentally whip out your five or six pre-prepared questions that you've practiced on other attendees. Go for gold.

- **Do ask your (rehearsed) question from the floor.** You've done the prep and you won't want to waste it. By having your question planned in advance, you will feel far more confident and prepared to put your hand up; you'll be less likely to be beaten to the punch by someone else asking a similar question first; and you will be the one that others admire later and wonder how on earth you did so well to think of such a smart question so quickly. Give it a try. Years ago, when someone said that I would need to be a speaker, I rubbished the idea because I was so nervous when speaking in public. I put my training wheels on for a full year before I launched by asking questions from the floor. It's great training.

4. Post event wrap up

- **Send a 'thank you' note afterwards**. This is brilliant, and I learned it from the best of the best when attending lots of conference in the US. In the US, when you meet someone at a business networking event, you nearly always get an email follow up to thank you. WOW! The first time it happened I was blown away because this is extremely uncommon in Australia. In fact, it's so uncommon in Australia that I recommend ensuring you keep a *light touch* so you don't come across as creepy. Say thanks, acknowledge something about them, and suggest that if they need anything they can drop you a line. Then a few weeks later, follow up with a phone or coffee meeting request. Avoid being too intense, avoid the too-soon sales pitch, and avoid coming across as needy. Instead, focus on how you can help them and keep conversations open down the track.

- **Review the plan**. Be sure to reflect on the events that gave you most value. Measure them against the *right people, right place, right messages and right time* criteria and you'll be futureproofing your career in no time.
- **Share the insights**. We've already discussed the plan, so create a report, a LinkedIn update, a staff meeting or intranet update. Don't keep your event attendance or the insights a secret.

There you have it: my top tips for helping you survive and thrive at networking events. It's all in the strategy. There is real benefit for you at these events. Make sure you are visible; start displaying your personal brand, your interest in career development and advancement, and your willingness to do something about it yourself.

Conferences: speaking and panels

Three steps to be a female kick ass speaker:

1. Be female
2. Speak
3. Then get onstage and go and kick some ass.

What are your best ideas for winning speaking gigs or panel gigs at conferences and events?

To win speaking opportunities, you need to put yourself forward. No more waiting for speaking opportunities to find you. Contact the organisers of the events where you want to speak and offer to speak. I encourage my executive clients to have two to three topic outlines, plus a draft speaker bio crafted in advance, in case they are asked or need to provide in a rush. Doing this initial planning work is half the battle. Working out what you stand for, how you add value and what that might look like in a 30-minute presentation will make you look like a Rockstar even if you're shaking at the knees. When, and only when, you have been accepted should you do the work and prepare your presentation. For the initial contacts, you just need a bio and a few summary topics that might entice.

If you're just starting out, instead of offering to speak, offer to be on a panel. Once again, be prepared in advance. Panels are great because they are short, conversational, and it's rare you need to do a presentation. In fact, it's usually discouraged. The panellists often get to bounce ideas off each other in advance and it's a lot less work. You also receive the same promotion and exposure as you would if you had delivered a 60-minute keynote—for 2% of the effort.

Case study (thinking outside the square when it comes to landing speaking gigs)

Jayne owns a highly successful architectural firm in a niche market. She decided to start building her own brand separate from the company brand by speaking at conferences and blogging via her company email newsletter and LinkedIn. Wow! She went from strength to strength with one of her articles being picked up by an international magazine and she won a speaking spot on an international conference program.

However, the speaking spot did not happen by chance. She created it. She identified a conference in Singapore which she wanted to attend. She contacted the organisers and explained that she understood that often speakers pulled out at the last minute. She was planning on attending anyway and had a couple of case studies up her sleeve that she could easily present at the last minute. Sure enough, a conference speaker pulled out and she got a gig—on stage, at the international industry conference of her choice. Yes, she had to pay to be there but the exposure for her business was significant and it helped build her positioning as an international thought leader in her industry.

Awards: to nominate or not, that is the question?

What does *Peppa Pig* have to do with a legal awards ceremony?

Well, heaps if you are one of the **#winning #women** doing the **#juggle** as they deliver excellence in Australian legal services. Celebrating and recognising excellence and achievement from women in any industry is a powerful driver towards gender equity.

I was absolutely chuffed to support **Gabrielle Guthrie** as she was named a finalist in the Sole Practitioner category at the Women in Law Awards hosted by *Lawyers Weekly* at the Sofitel in November 2019. I was so proud of her results and achievements in just two years of establishing her own practice providing accessible, specialist environment and planning law advice. Phenomenal woman. Phenomenal lawyer. Phenomenal result

The 21 acceptance speeches represented all the richness, value and **#diversity** that working women provide to society with many reflecting that, despite the juggle, they were still able to deliver substantive change or results for clients. One winner explained that she submitted her award nomination video only to realise later that *Peppa Pig* was playing in the background of the submission. It may just have swayed the judges.

Kudos to all the 180 finalists in the room and to the 20 women who were named as #winners.

Keep inspiring others.

Awards are a great way to stand out

Let's take a further step back. Doing the preparation and planning required to nominate for an award is almost as good as winning an award. Nominating for an award can feel like a lot hard work. But most people who do the preparation for the nomination process, tell me they feel better off purely as a result of the process.

There is something quite liberating about categorising and sorting through a heap of effort, progress and outcomes to create a compelling narrative. Most of us achieve a lot in the day-to-day of work, but we are also the first to brush it off with 'oh it was nothing, just my job'. However, when you spend time writing about your achievements in a business case or award methodology, all of a sudden, you can see that no, this isn't just your job, in fact, you've achieved something substantial. Clients frequently tell me that developing the nomination in a systematic way, perhaps in collaboration with the communications team, someone from marketing or an award writing consultant, can be just the boost they need to reach a little higher up the pipeline.

In most instances, you'll need quantifiable or qualifiable evidence to demonstrate change. Think about before and after weight loss photos. We love them. We love seeing how someone worked hard to become healthy. It's the same with awards judging panels. They need to see before and after metrics or some sort of evidence to help ensure the business case for brand you is a winning submission. Many women don't collect this data. We've frequently come up through the ranks via disciplines that are 'softer' and don't have direct P&L impact. Until that changes, the earlier in your career you can start collecting quantifiable hard data evidence, the smoother your ascendancy to the C-suite will be. Plus you may just win an award along the way.

LinkedIn tips for award finalists and winners

- Take a photo. If someone can capture a photo of you actually winning (not posing) even better. Add it to your photo collage.
- Announce your win or place on LinkedIn. You don't need to do it on the night. In fact, given that so few people are on LinkedIn in the late evening, you're best to save it for the next day.
- When you do announce it, avoid the socialised tendency to start with 'I'm so humbled to have received this award'. That's a given. By starting that way, all you'll be remembered for is being nice and humble. Instead, start with a statement about why you received the award, something about your expertise, what you stand for or a position you've taken with

your speciality—your 'why'. Then, and only then, segue into how delighted or humbled you are and thank those who supported you.

Other tips for winners and finalists

- Invite your boss along to the awards ceremony. In fact, get your boss to host a table and pay. I've heard stories of women keeping this stuff a secret in case they don't win. Well, most people don't win. But being in the awards is significant enough. Bring your boss and team along on the journey. They'll be your cheer squad and may be even more supportive next year.
- Add it to your resume. Don't be shy. Remember the award is not the only achievement here, the award is validation of your credibility building.
- Add it to your LinkedIn profile in the awards section.
- Also, if it's mentioned in the press, add a hyperlink or a photo of the event in the media section of your summary.
- Winners: see if you can generate some press (industry press is great for this). Get the communications team to help. You don't need to go it alone. Yes, it is worth it. In a highly competitive talent market, organisations like to be known as places that allow winners to flourish.

Associations and peak bodies

In my book *Step Up, Speak Out, Take Charge,* I dedicated almost an entire chapter to taking advantage of your professional association. Given my own 20-year career history in the sector, I'm pretty passionate about how helpful a proactive approach to your membership association can be. I've seen junior members elevate themselves in industry far more easily because they spent time building a profile outside of their organisation by investing in their professional association. Once again, the key is to be a proactive (not just a passive) user of the membership.

Offer to help, offer to advise, volunteer to go above and beyond, be clear about what you can and can't do—then do it.

A word of warning to those who do get involved: don't just get yourself on the events social committee. Get yourself on the conference or curriculum programming committee. However, if the social events committee is your only option, start there ... then move onto another committee after your first year. Why? You don't want to get pigeonholed as an event's organiser. There's nothing wrong with an event's organiser; I am one. However, the impact of events work is diminished by the assumption you're some kind of party planner—and that's dismissed as the Player.

 Case study (leveraging your peak body)

Jessica is a young professional who works in the technology space. Sometimes people take her for granted and overlook her opinion because she is young, female and attractive in a masculine-dominated industry. Yet she is highly educated, driven, motivated and is keen to see more women succeed in technology. She started building a brand for herself via the national peak body. While at times in her professional career she was overlooked or her contribution pigeonholed, this was not the case for the peak body.

Most recently, she was voted President for Victoria for the 2nd term. As a result, she now has a huge profile in the industry; she speaks at and MCs events; she champions gender diversity; she has been featured on *Women's Agenda,* is a voice for change for women in technology and has just completed the *Australian Institute of Company Directors* course with a view to landing paid board work in the future.

Don't dismiss the power of your peak body for giving your career a boost.

CHAPTER 9

LINKEDIN FOR SELF PROMOTION

I didn't know how to express my opinion on LinkedIn.

I was scared. 'What if I get it wrong? What if I end up with trolls? 'What if people don't agree with me?'

When I found my sense of purpose, something surprising happened. The more of an authentic position I took, the more my posts resonated, the more my clients and readers messaged me and … the easier it all became.

Boom!

I realised that you don't need to be right, to be the funniest or the best to express your opinion on LinkedIn. But you do need to be able to articulate your position. Not simply regurgitate the opinion of others. Why?

- People connect with people.
- People 'buy' from people they like and identify with.
- Your unique perspective will resonate with your tribe.

One of the most powerful opportunities for busy executives is to brand themselves via LinkedIn. This will help you stand out in a crowd and ensure you are memorable even when you are head down backside up solving complex business problems.

So embrace your inner expert:

1. What do you stand for?

2. Why is that important?

3. How does it add value?

Then let go of 'busy, right and perfect', and give yourself permission to have your say.

Why LinkedIn?

It's a new world out there. Social selling, social influence and social persuasion are new areas of leadership expertise. They drive engagement, build trust, increase transparency and give power back to those who are skilled in it. And anyone can learn.

Leaders of the future will not run scared as they will have mastered social selling and platform profile building.

LinkedIn is a powerful social media platform to leverage because your three biggest stakeholders are already on there: customers, shareholders and staff—each of past, current and future. Anyone with leadership aspirations or a drive to make a difference is missing the boat if they think they can avoid building a brand and leveraging via social selling and persuasion strategies.

Why? Because consumers trust individuals over brands and institutions.

> CEO social engagement is a reputational must today. Business leaders are increasingly turning to digital platforms to share their company story, reach broader networks of stakeholders and join online conversations where their company is already being talked

about. CEOs who don't embrace online communications risk being left behind.—**Leslie Gaines-Ross,** Chief Reputation Strategist, *Weber Shandwick*

If you have C-suite, leadership or consultancy aspirations, social media engagement is a must. If you don't embrace online communications, you risk being left behind. But how to go about it?

Like most, you probably set up a LinkedIn account at some point in the mid-late 2000s, then promptly forgot about it. Maybe you updated it a little with your most recent role change, or perhaps you leave it to your executive or virtual assistant to manage. Most people underestimate the power of LinkedIn, and quite simply, are leaving money and opportunity on the table. While you might be getting away with it currently, this will become a risk to you in the future as more social media savvy generation Ys and Zs, move further up the food chain.

Using LinkedIn effectively takes skill and effort at first but it's worth it. Once you become a confident, savvy user, you can make it work for you. Once again, take charge of the narrative before it takes charge of you. Or in the case of LinkedIn, why not get on the front foot and start creating the narrative, instead of being a passive consumer.

Common mistakes

If you have some experience with LinkedIn but are not yet confident enough to fully engage, you might recognise yourself in one of these categories:

- **The Loser**. You have less than 100 connection; you've never heard of the *500+ connections unwritten ground rule* and it's obvious you'd really rather not be on LinkedIn.

- **The Near Enough is Good Enough**. Your profile pic is a selfie, or a glamour shot, or it looks like you cut your significant other out of the photo and any of your LinkedIn activity is by happy accident rather than by design.
- **The Online Catalogue**. You think of your profile purely as an online resume (not a very good one at that) and you're playing a passive waiting game.
- **The Cheer Squad**. You limit your involvement to random 'thumbs up' and 'great article' comments, and you wistfully observe others who comment confidently.
- **The Stalker**. You passively read articles and view profiles in the background, maybe even with your identity hidden.
- **The Now You See Me, Now You Don't**. You are super active in fits and starts, but when work gets busy, you play least in sight. You try anything once or twice but with no plan, no system and no strategy.
- **The Squeaky Wheel**. You're on a mission with articles you like, share and publish. You clearly articulate a problem set but you never offer solutions.
- **The Automator**. Someone once told you about a software automated solution to help you share content on LinkedIn. So, that's all you do. You haven't realised the benefits others are gaining by using a more tailored, engaging and personalised approach to connection. And buyer beware: while many sharing software and automating solutions are fine, messaging and connection software may be breaching LinkedIn guidelines; therefore, spending a week or two in LinkedIn Jail is a very real possibility.
- **The Dominator**. Where you dominate the feed morning, noon or night, leaving others questioning *when do you fit work in?* You begin to wonder why your post engagement is dropping. You've never heard the phrase 'leave them wanting more'.

Ultimately though, we're aiming for **The LinkedIn Ninja status aka the Linked-Ninja:**

- You have fine-tuned your social selling abilities and execute them effectively, efficiently and with ease.
- You understand that LinkedIn is predominantly about building engagement, trust and rapport, so all your efforts are nuanced, coordinated and graceful.

By way of metrics, you have:

- A top 1% viewed profile in both your industry and in your network.
- A social selling index of 75%+ (check it out www.linkedin.com/sales/ssi/).
- 3000+ connections with a repeatable plan for both engaging with those connections and growing new connections in the direction of your goals.
- An average viewing rate on shares of 5000+.
- A *thumbs up* rating on posts and shares averages 50+.
- An average of 300+ viewing/eyeball rate on published articles.
- Branded or themed activity and in alignment with your long-term goals.
- A game behind the game: a long-term goal you hope to achieve with LinkedIn as just one part of the plan.

Strategic approach to building your profile

'If your work isn't online, it doesn't exist.'

—Austin Kleon, Show Your Work

If a tree falls in the forest does anyone see it? If a girl works back late in the office, does anyone know? And if your profile doesn't turn up on page one or two of the search results for your subject matter expertise, then you may as well be in outer Siberia. There are entire books dedicated to LinkedIn profile writing; however, LinkedIn algorithms are constantly changing, so I've highlighted a few areas to help you get more benefit than what the standard advice offers.

The biggest mistake most of us make is to think of our profile as an online resume. Just like an Aldi catalogue, we pack it with everything that's in store—all the sellout specials and end-of-line runouts. Instead, think of your profile as the shop window of a prestigious department store, working 24/7 for you. Just because you don't go on LinkedIn very much, doesn't mean that others don't or that they're not looking at your profile and making assumptions about you. Or worse, that they can't find your profile so also make assumptions about you.

Don't underestimate your profile build. Perception is 9/10ths of the law. It matters.

Take control of LinkedIn, before it takes control of you

For those who are nervous about LinkedIn, be sure to take control of your **settings and privacy.**

This is critical in terms of you spending less time on things that aren't important and keeping you protected. Invest 30 minutes to get familiar and take control now; it will pay you back in spades in the future. (In the top right hand corner, under the tiny photo of you, there is a drop-down box. Be sure to head on in and check out the three tabs within the **settings and privacy** area. Work through it line by line so you understand.)

LinkedIn is constantly making changes to its **settings and privacy**. Make yourself familiar and review regularly.

Do you have All-star Status?

The grey dashboard on your profile should tell you what's missing. If you don't have All-star Status, work out what's missing and add it in. It also tells you:

1. How many people have viewed your profile in the last three months?

2. How many people have looked at your last share?

3. How many searches you have come up in.

This helps you draw a line in the sand and work out where you can get some easy wins. Have you filled out all areas of your profile? Are people looking at your profile? What words are they finding you for? Are people engaging with your shares? What gets measured gets done. Keep an eye on your results.

Turn it off

- Turn the 'update people about the changes to your profile' button to OFF. Leave it set to OFF until just before you want to strategically announce something such as new role, a board or committee appointment or a volunteer opportunity.

Then, switch it ON for a week, then off again after you've dealt with all the well wishes.

- Turn off any sounds or mobile alerts. The more people start taking notice of you, the more interfering it will become. Just program a time each day to log in and look at your profile—just like you would schedule in finances or something else at work.
- Consider switching off all emails from LinkedIn. It's a distraction and if you are going to be using it more professionally, the LinkedIn messaging option is enough.
- Consider keeping connections private, unless they are an asset.

Your photo

Having a professional photo shoot is now considered standard for any executive. Don't wait for someone to organise the shoot for you. Get it done. I suggest getting a new professional headshot every 3–4 years. Dress and have photos representing a super successful and professional you—for the role you want, not the role you have. Your photo needs to 'sell' success.

Connections and followers

500+ connections is the unwritten ground rule for an employee; 1500+ for a well-connected socially savvy business leader; and 3000+ connections in your area of expertise great for a consultant. Got more than that already? Don't let that stop you. Keep building out your network strategically in the direction of your choice. It's not only the number that matters (social proof), it's what you do with those connections that truly counts. Have a messaging strategy in place is for the truly advanced.

Shorten your LinkedIn URL

It's very easy and looks super professional. Read more here: https://www.linkedin.com/help/linkedin/answer/87/customizing-your-public-profile-url?lang=en

Summary

Do complete the summary area. Many people leave it empty and that's a waste. Ironically, this needs to be less about you and more about the problems you solve, the difference you make and the value you add. Why not make use of all the 2000 characters available? Don't simply *copy and paste* the front page of your resume unless it's been written with LinkedIn in mind. Consider your audience and write it for them.

Add some media or hyperlinks on your profile summary

Have you been featured in a magazine? Do you/your organisation have a website? Have you spoken at a conference? Do you have photos of you speaking at an event? Plug at least three things in your summary. It looks uber cool.

Roles and experience

Just like your resume, write one brief sentence about the scope of the role and the context of the organisation. List one, two, maybe three, achievements. Sell the sizzle, not the sausage. Use *future* focused content. Future brand you. Ironically, less is more. Don't list every job you've had since you left high school. Don't even list your high school unless you've just finished. Be strategic about the narrative you are creating; only list what's relevant to your current aspirations. Go back 10–15 years only.

Logos = credibility

Logos make you look more credible. Sometimes though, they don't appear when you type in the field for your career history. Perhaps the organisation has only recently established a LinkedIn page or changed its name. If a company logo (education and career history) is not coming up in the first instance, double check, re-enter and search again.

Recommendations ...

... are a must; otherwise, your profile won't rank despite best intentions. Minimum effective dose is three. Get three fast. The more the better. We live in an era of online reviews and word-of-mouth marketing. Recommendations are a great way to build credibility. Also, are your recommendations recent enough? I see quite a few clients who have recommendations for the work they did in 2014, but nothing since. This should be an activity you do every six months. Once you have your minimum of three, pick your people wisely. Do they add value to future brand you? Give your potential referee a few hints or bullet points as to what you want them to write. That way, there is less to-ing and fro-ing. Proactive and strategic is great; although, any are better than none.

Background photo

'A picture says a thousand words' so you are allowed to be creative here. Use this real estate to focus on building positioning and credibility. Beware the photos that make you look like you'd rather be on a beach or retired. Use a background image that enhances the perception of future brand you and makes your career strategy easier to execute.

Regularly review

Finally, review your profile every year. Does it need restructuring? Remember, LinkedIn algorithms change, as do your career goals, so what was working a year ago may not work a year later. Is it still pointing you in the direction of your choice and written with *future you* in mind? Does it need re-writing? Don't be shy. After all, a change is as good as a holiday ...

Strategic approach to building your network

Build a repeatable plan that will grow in the direction of your choice; focus on people who make you look good, people who can help you; people who might be your ideal clients/employer/future boss.

Remember the *Power up your networking* model? Build out your LinkedIn connections in the same way. I recommend four categories:

1. Low Hanging Fruit: the connections that LinkedIn suggests, or plug in your phone and synchronise your contacts. These people are more likely to accept because they already know you.

2. Amplifiers: possible connections who are influencers or recruiters; those with lots of connections or who might champion you in the future.

3. Future Direction: deliberately start building out your connections in the direction of your career goals.

4. Decision Makers: deliberately look for decision makers, division heads or business leaders more broadly and connect up.

Send a personal note where possible. It increases the chances of connection, especially when reaching out to those who don't know you or if the connection is important to you. Connect with future career and leadership goals front of mind.

 Case study (LinkedIn Award Winner)

Jayne is an amazingly strategic woman. Like many, she can be a little nervous at networking functions, so she took to LinkedIn like a duck to water as it enabled her to network without leaving her office. Using the approach above, she grew her network on LinkedIn and scheduled time each day to reach out using the criteria above. Every day, she sent 25–30 connection requests, and personalised the note where possible.

She proactively managed any unaccepted invitations through the invitation center; therefore, after a week or so, if someone hadn't responded to her request, she would withdraw the request so she could resend at a later date. This assisted her to keep under the invitation cap that LinkedIn imposes. She also used the *Power up your networking* model to assess how she responded to invitations to connect. Remember, more is not necessarily better but perception matters.

As a result of her strategic efforts, Jayne landed a new role **and** was promoted within three months of landing that role. Plus she grew her online network 3000+ connections in just three months and 8K connections in a year.

In 2017, Jayne was awarded with a LinkedIn Power Profile in her industry sector (and again in 2018). This led to many speaking opportunities and being profiled in industry magazines and interviewed on podcasts. All these things are profile and credibility building activities.

Jayne's advice? Learn to love LinkedIn as it's a powerful profile building tool for those who feel stuck in the office with no time for networking.

Take a strategic approach to publishing and posting

'Raise your visibility by consistently writing about topics that matter to both you and your audiences.'

—Nancy Ancowitz

Align your posting, sharing and publishing with your career goals. Share best practice industry, leadership and management tips in your sector or within the sector to which you are moving. Don't wait until you get there, that's almost too late.

Be aware that others read between the lines of your work. Sarah was desperately unhappy in her role and organisation; however, she wasn't in a position to move on. Unfortunately, every time she shared on LinkedIn, we all got a sense of her unhappiness at work because she shared articles about:

- The impact of poor culture on retention of employees and staff happiness.
- What to do when the leadership team has lost the plot.
- How to handle bad managers.

Sarah wasn't an HR executive so it gave away the fact she was unhappy; instead, she could have been sharing about best practice in her own domain and how it adds value, or highlighting great company cultures.

Case study

Keli worked in her organisation for a long time and she wanted to reinvent herself. She wrote her ideal job description and started looking for roles that fit. She found a role, in an organisation she greatly admired, that was in a slightly different area to most of her recent career. This didn't stop her. She was smart in her use of LinkedIn and how she tipped the perception in her favour while sharing.

She regularly and consistently shared articles and 'think pieces' that were more about the technical expertise of the role for which she was applying. She knew her strategy worked because she landed the role and her profile was looked at several times during the recruitment process by people from the potential organisation. In fact, during the interview, one of the panelists commented on a recent share.

'It's probably easier for you to write about yourself than talk about yourself. Did you get a promotion at work? Or is your new blog taking off? Post about it and don't feel ashamed.'

—Jean Granneman

Quick and easy essential posting ideas

- When you are leaving your organisation, alert your network with an upbeat, friendly announcement that gives thanks and credit.
- Alert your network shortly after you start a new role with a photo and a similar post, but more about your new direction. Thank (and tag) your new team for a great welcome.

- Summarise research articles that spark your interest. I like HBR, Inc., and Gartner. Be the meaning maker so that your network doesn't have to.
- Share about a key collaborative project, take a photo, make it fun.
- Alert your network after 100 days or even one year, in the new organisation, with key learnings.

Take a strategic approach to messaging

Messaging is one of the most under-utilised sections of LinkedIn for executives. If you're a Fixer by nature and like to fly a little under the radar, then messaging is definitely for you.

LinkedIn messaging, in its current form, is just that—messaging. In the old days, it was emailing that led to more formal notes. This newer, lighter messaging style means that disarming, gracious and personalised tones are key to your messaging strategy that builds rapid rapport, trust and buy in. Here are my key tips for messaging:

1. **Be strategic**

   Have a hit list of people on LinkedIn aligned with the four quadrants of the *Power up your networking* model, and send them messages on a consistent (but not too frequent) basis.

2. **Once every few months try one of the following messages**

   Here's an article thought you may like. I know of your interest in X Y Z.

   Here's a recent article I wrote. Given your area of expertise, would you like to comment?

   I saw you on the XYC Industry Conference program: great topic. Wish I could have been there. Will you be presenting anywhere else?

Next time you're in town I'd love to buy you a coffee to talk about XYZ. Let me know in advance.

Plus, if you've got time, also send the regular congratulations notes that LinkedIn suggest to acknowledge birthdays, anniversaries and new roles.

3. **Personalise where you can**

Personalisation can come in many forms:

Make sure your notes or emails read as though you've written it specifically for the recipient.
Use their first name.
Correct spelling is really important.
Demonstrate that you've read something in their profile (industry, company, career history, or even better, something they've recently shared/written/commented on). For example, if you are sending an article to someone, make sure it's relevant; if asking for a meeting, make sure it's relevant.

4. **Biggest personalisation fails …**

Great article (insert first name). Yes we've all received canned messages like this. We may even have sent one or two in our attempts to copy, paste and scale. Handle with caution and avoid at all costs. If your error rate is high, simply don't add their name in.

5. **Disarming** (so as not to overwhelm or raise objections before you start a conversation)

Start with some sort of sentiment that puts them at ease.
Keep it conversational.
Use regular language.
Be non-confrontational.
Don't be needy.

Don't use too much jargon.
Don't go straight into a sales pitch.
Don't use a huge chunk of text that looks like a copy and paste.
Keep it brief.

6. **Be gracious**

Offer to help.
Acknowledge them for the connection request or for connecting.
Invite them to drop you a note if they need anything.
Suggest they Direct Message (DM) if you can help with introductions or information.
Ask them to get in touch if they'd like assistance with (insert the problem you solve).
Thank them for the connection note. Tell them you appreciate their personal note because it's so rare in this day and age.

 Case study (Example of a recent connection note)

Hi Marie

I hope you are well. Great to connect.

I've been having fun on LinkedIn recently. In fact, one of my clients (who was acknowledged with a 2017 LinkedIn Power Profile) has recently challenged me to see who can get to 10K connections first. Thanks for helping me get a little closer to my 10K.

If you are in the business of creating a movement (not a ripple), then this article will help http://www.amandablesing.com/blog/2017/9/21/the-power-of-authentic-voice

If there is anything I can help with, please drop me a note.

Keep in touch

Amanda

Simply schedule

Consistency trumps frequency. Have a schedule and stick to it until it's time to review or you get feedback that it's not working any more. Remember: right audience, right key messages, right time, right place in the right currency—you can't go wrong.

FINAL WORD

Self-promotion, whether you like it or not, is an essential part of your executive toolkit. After all, how will others know of the results or impact you have made in the past (and how they might help in the future) if you don't tell them?

For busy executives who still struggle with self-promotion, learning to get out of your own way or putting mechanisms in place to help you take the 'self' out of self-promotion will be your fast-track to success.

For executive women in particular, until there is closer to 50% of women in leadership, you also need to navigate the bias, preconceived ideas and stereotypes on your journey to the top. It may not feel fair or easy but it will make your pathway smoother.

Along with the eight pillars of self-promotion, executive women may also want to leverage the feminine leadership superpowers (also stereotyped) of active listening, clear communication and emotional intelligence, which are powerful tools in negotiation.

REFERENCES

Artz, B., Goodall, A., & Oswald, A. J. (2018). Research: Women ask for raises as often as men, but are less likely to get them. *Harvard Business Review*. Retrieved from https://hbr.org/2018/06/research-women-ask-for-raises-as-often-as-men-but-are-less-likely-to-get-them

Barlow, J., & Moller, C. (2008). *A complaint is a gift: Using feedback as a strategic tool*. Berrett-Koehler Publishers.

Blesing, A. (2016). *Step up, speak out, take charge: A woman's guide to getting ahead in your career*.

Bureau of labor statistics. (2017). Retrieved from https://www.bls.gov/news.release/pdf/nlsoy.pdf

Clark, T. (2011). *Nerve: Poise under pressure, serenity under stress, and the brave new sciences of fear and cool*. Little, Brown and Company.

Coffman, J., & Neuenfeldt, B. (2014). *Eveyday moments of truth: Frontline managers are key to women's career aspirations*. Bain & Company. Retrieved from https://www.bain.com/insights/everyday-moments-of-truth/

Dweck, C. S. (2017). *Mindset: Changing the way you think to fulfil your potential*. Robinson.

Entrepreneurs, H. (2013). *Self-promotion sucks (but it doesn't have to)*. Hungry Entrepreneurs.

Fang, Y., Frqancis, B., & Hasan, I. (2018). Research: CEOs with diverse networks create higher firm value. *Harvard Business review*. Retrieved from https://hbr.org/2018/04/research-ceos-with-diverse-networks-create-higher-firm-value

Gan, M., Heller, D., & Chen, S. (2018). The power in being yourself: Feeling authentic enhances the sense of power. *Personality and Social Psychology Bulletin*. Retrieved from https://journals. sagepub.com/doi/abs/10.1177/0146167218771000

Ibarra, H., Ely, R. J., & Kolb, D. M. (2013). Women rising: The unseen barriers. *Harvard Business Review*. Retrieved from https://hbr. org/2013/09/women-rising-the-unseen-barriers

Johnson, S. K., & Hekman, D. R. (2016). Women and minorities are penalised fro promoting diversity. *Harvard Business Review*. Retrieved from https://hbr.org/2016/03/women-and-minorities-are-penalized-for-promoting-diversity

Kay, K., & Shipman, C. (2014). *The confidence code: The science and art of self-assurance - what women should know*. HarperBusiness.

Korn Ferry. (2018). *Women CEOs speak*. Korn Ferry. Retrieved from https://www.kornferry.com/perspective-women-leaders-of-the-future

KPMG. (2018). *Global CEO outlook 2018: Australia*. KPMG. Retrieved from https://home.kpmg.com/au/en/home/insights/2018/05/global-ceo-outlook-2018-australia.html

KPMG. (2019). *For women at work, risk taking has rewards, yet many hesitate to leap into the unfamiliar*. Retrieved from KPMG: https://home.kpmg/us/en/home/media/press-releases/2019/01/for-women-at-work-risk-taking-has-rewards-yet-many-hesitate-to-leap-into-the-unfamiliar.html

Larkins, F. (2018). *Male students remain underrepresented in Australian universities. Should we be concerned?* Retrieved from The University of Melbourne: https://melbourne-cshe. unimelb.edu.au/lh-martin-institute/insights/gender-enrolment-trends-flarkins

Moss-Racusin, C. A., & Rudman, L. A. (2010). Disruptions in women's self-promotion: The backlash avoidance model. *Psychology of*

Women Quarterly. Retrieved from https://journals.sagepub.com/doi/abs/10.1111/j.1471-6402.2010.01561.x

Orbach, S. (2006). *Fat is a feminist issue*. Arrow.

Smith, J. L., & Huntoon, M. (2013). Women's bragging rights: Overcoming modesty norms to facilitate women's self-promotion. *Psychology of Women Quarterly*. Retrieved from https://hbr.org/2016/03/women-and-minorities-are-penalized-for-promoting-diversity

Tate, C. (2017). *The purpose project: A handbook for bringing meaning to life at work*.

The institute of leadership & management. (n.d.). *Ambition and gender at work*. The institute of leadership & management.

Weber Shandwick. (2015). *The CEO reputationpremium: A new era of engagement*. Retrieved from Weber Shandwick : https://www.webershandwick.com/news/the-ceo-reputation-premium-a-new-era-of-engagement/